THE
WELLNESS CENTER SOLUTION:

How Physicians Can Transform Their Practices, Their Income, and Their Lives

BY DR. RAJ GUPTA

Library of Congress Control Number: 2017937458

Paperback: 978-0-692-86417-3
Hardcover: 978-0-692-86656-6

Book design by Michelle Manley

The doctor of the future will give no medication, but will interest his patients in the care of the human frame, diet and in the cause and prevention of disease.

—Thomas A. Edison

MISSION STATEMENT:

To help as many people as possible avoid unnecessary medication and unnecessary surgery through diet and exercise and the services provided at our Soul Focus Wellness Center.

ABOUT THE AUTHOR:

The founder and the creator of the Soul Focus Wellness Center franchise, Dr. Raj A. Gupta, obtained a marketing degree from Drexel University and then attended Chiropractic school at Life Chiropractic College, graduating in 1996. Dr. Gupta believes that overall health comes from D.R.E.A.M, which is equal management of Diet, Rest, Exercise, and both mechanical (Adjustments) and Mental stability. He is passionate about, and has dedicated his life, to health, wellness, and preventative healthcare. Dr. Gupta exposes the flaws of the current "sick care" model and challenges patients to adopt "healthcare" as a lifestyle. Dr. Gupta enjoys working out, playing tennis, going to the beach, driving fast cars, and listening to classic rock and roll. He adores his two girls to whom he refers as "his princesses."

DEDICATION

I would like to dedicate this book to my parents, Barbara and Anand Gupta. Thank you Mom for my perseverance and confidence, and thank you Dad for my work ethic and drive. I continue to work hard to make you both proud. Dad, wish you were here. Darsh, looking forward to our life together, thank you for all your love and support. To my new baby, I cannot wait to meet you! A special thank you to my sister, Rachel, and my two children, Asha and Abigail, for your patience and support in allowing me to pursue my D.R.E.A.M.

ACKNOWLEDGEMENTS

Dr. David Singer, Dr. Gagandeep Gill, Mark DeEulio, Kathleen Flynn, Dr. Alan Stern and George, (Skip) Bariscillo and my colleagues in my Master Mind Group.

Thank you all for your support, guidance, and undying dedication to me and Soul Focus.

CONTENTS

CHAPTER ONE

You Take Care of Everybody Else's Pain — But What about Your Own?

Doctors have it made, right? We get respect, we own practices and live life on our terms, and we, of course, make lots of money. At least, that is the general consensus among laypeople. However, as most of us have learned firsthand, physicians know the truth. The truth is that the medical profession is in crisis and the whole system is under strain. Doctors are now putting in more hours and making less than ever before, hardly able to keep up with bills, dues, and payments on their student loans. Gone are the days when going to medical school meant that you had it made.

Most people don't go to medical school for the money. They don't do it for the prestige. They go to medical school because *they genuinely want to be doctors.* They dream of one day opening their own practice and having their own patients. Like all people, we just want to serve and lead the good life. We just want the same

American Dream as anyone else while keeping our communities healthy enough to achieve the same.

But for too many physicians practicing today, this dream is anything but a reality. Physicians across the nation are waking up to an American Nightmare. They thought that medical school was the ticket to the good, easy life. They thought it was a way to earn a good living while also serving the community. However, what they are discovering is that it has never been harder to make a good living as a doctor. In fact, it is getting harder each and every year. This, in turn, makes it increasingly difficult to serve your community.

That's a triple-lose situation. Community health systems are eroding. Patients are paying more money for a lower quality of care. Doctors are struggling to get by in a way that they shouldn't have to after ten or more years of higher education and the smothering debt that comes with it.

No one wins here. We all lose.

I DIDN'T SIGN UP FOR *THIS*—DID I?

If you picked up this book, you probably already know what it's like owning your own practice today. You thought that you'd be making the big bucks once you got through medical school and residency.

What's more, you didn't think you would have to struggle. It is thought that referrals will come in from other doctors, especially for specialists, and that the insurance company will take care of reimbursement. Historically, this has been the case, yet reimbursements are down and insurance companies seem to change what they are willing to cover every month. You're constantly getting calls and emails that this service, that medicine, this treatment is no long covered under the patients plan.

Even if insurance is willing to pay for services, your patients still have to be able to afford them, and this is becoming harder each day. Most insurance companies incentivize patients to go to in-network doctors by offering plans with high out-of-network deductibles. This can result in out-of-pocket expenses that may be well in excess of $3,000-5,000. I once had a patient with a $46,000 out-of-pocket deductible! Additionally, patients are feeling this squeeze too. Most health coverage plans now have in-network deductibles too, something never seen before! If patients cannot afford to pay their out of pocket expense, they're going to the cheaper in-network providers whether they want to or not.

You may be tempted to join an HMO and become an in-network provider, but the insurance company negotiates very low, predetermined rates for in-network providers. In order to keep your income from falling, you have to see four or five in-network patients for every one out-of-network patient you used to see. You end up working harder to make the same amount. There are only two alternatives in this situation—either you accept the rate and the additional work hours it entails or you stay an out-of-network provider running your own practice. Neither choice currently yields an optimum solution to your dilemma.

Unfortunately, physicians running their own practices, refusing to join an HMO and accept the stipulations that go along with being in-network, often see their volume of patients and total reimbursement going down year after year. They're trying to maintain their practices, but aren't getting ahead. They're asking themselves: "Now what? How do I make a living after I have invested my life's work and hundreds or thousands of dollars on my education?"

If you're not willing to join an HMO, only one answer presents itself: get more patients. Patients are the lifeblood of a practice. They are essential to generating new business. They are the new business. The only way to bring in more money when the insurance companies are reducing reimbursements is to increase patient volume. Assuming you can even find enough patients able and willing to pay their out of pocket expenses and meet their out-of-network deductibles—and that's a big if—you're still working harder seeing more patients. In order to do this, you have to work longer hours—often much longer. You start taking patients in the office six to seven days a week, week in and week out. You're pulling ten-hour shifts regularly, longer if things get busier. And that's just the time you spend with patients. Running a practice means running a business. There are administrative responsibilities, staff management, executive duties. Before you know it, you're easily racking up eighty hours a week. Suddenly your take-home pay, when you break it down by hour, doesn't look so good. You start to envy all your friends who studied computer science who have cushy forty-hour-per-week jobs as programmers. Even your friends in finance and big law jobs seem to be working fewer hours than you—and they paid off their student loans ten years ago!

Around all of this you need to squeeze in yearly continuing education credits. You end up spending your vacation time in order to attend several education seminars just to keep your license.

The work is nonstop. It's a raging river bearing down on you. You look forward to weekends not for leisure, but to finally catch up on the administrative work you need to do on the practice. Weekdays you're too busy taking patients. You can't start catching up on notes, paying bills, doing the books, and business planning until Saturday. Most of the weekend, you spend trying to cut expenses. You're always trying to cut expenses.

The first thing you do after waking up isn't brushing your teeth. It's not coffee. Okay, maybe it is coffee, if it helps you trudge to the computer to check your bank accounts. You want to be sure all your payments cleared and you haven't bounced a check. It's a struggle just keeping the practice in the black. Payroll is an issue. Overhead is an issue. You have to make tough choices about which personnel to keep. You're always pinching pennies around the office, sometimes for things as simple as office supplies.

You're asking yourself, how did it come to this? Sure, you're a physician and you're getting by. You're even making good money by objective standards. But you're not thriving. You didn't spend ten years in medical school and go hundreds of thousands of dollars into debt just to get by. You owe hundreds of thousands of dollars for medical school, probably have undergraduate loans, and racked up living expenses for ten years of schooling. You can be half a million dollars in debt easily by the time you open your practice. There's no escape button. You can't discharge your student loan debt. You can't let the practice go under because your employees and patients are all counting on you.

You might have been okay with it if you were just making what you made last year—but you're making less. And next year you'll be making even less. And there's nothing you can do about it except turn the wheels harder, see more and more patients. The insurance companies keep cutting reimbursements.

All of this is taking its toll. You can't sleep. You're always worried about where the next patient is coming from. Your reimbursements are going down. There are delays in reimbursements. (Sometimes they take a year to come in—that's happened to me on numerous occasions.) You're working constantly, with little time to spend with friends and family. Your spouse feels like they are becoming a stranger to you, as you miss your children's birthdays and sports games. You cannot remember the last time you had a moment to yourself or your hobbies. All you have time for is work.

The financial pressures of the office, let alone your personal life, can be too much to bear. If you have kids early, you may be wondering how you're ever going to send them to good colleges. How will you pay for their education when you're still paying off your own?

It's not just your own family either. You're also worried about your employees and their families. You don't want to let anyone down. You don't want to let good employees go—but where is the money going to come from? When things get tight, you have to start cutting staff.

Often the first people let go are doctors working under you. You can't answer your own phones or book appointments, but you can take more patients, and cutting a doctor's salary can save you six figures. This can be attractive in the short term, but in the long run it just means more work for you. You think you will double up and skip lunch breaks to make it work, but the quality of your work goes down and you may even start losing patients or getting bad online reviews.

You may not have to worry about letting staff go—they may leave you. Staff turnover is high in most medical practices today. Due to less money from reimbursements, doctors can't afford to compensate their employees as well as they used to, which can lead to attrition. However, your employees do not blame the insurance companies, they blame you. It may not be your fault, but you can't really blame them for heading to greener pastures. Sometimes you look around your practice and start longing to join them!

All the while, the vultures are circling. You have practice management gurus knocking on your door. Do you need help? Do you need an office manager? Do you need "consultants"? These people want the last slice of the little bit of pie you have left.

At a certain point, it becomes more than you can handle. Many doctors are left asking themselves: "How did my life turn out this way?" This is a worthy recognition and a valid question. But these are the two questions you should be asking yourself:

"How did I get here?"

And, "What can I do to get out?"

Many practice owners are almost ready to do the unthinkable: join an HMO.

This is a deal with the devil for doctors who are accustomed to running their own independent practices. It means signing your rights away. When you join an HMO, you are the doctor in name only. The insurance company is in charge of making decisions about patient care. Manage-care doctors must give approval for anything that is done. They make choices that are in line with the interests of the insurance company, not the doctor or patient. This is untenable for most doctors. What kind of doctor doesn't get the last word on patient care? The sad truth is this: most doctors working today.

Some physicians sell their practices to local hospitals for a lump sum of money and then become employees at their own practice. While this pays off debt, relieves stress, and allows the doctor to put some money in the bank, the lump sum is not enough to retire on. You end up as an employee being told how to run the practice you built, and you don't have the retirement money to walk away with.

But what else can you do? The lack of options has many practice owners effectively giving up the keys to their practices. It's hard, but the sad fact is that it has become impossible to run a small medical practice in today's current climate in America, so more and more doctors are turning away from their practices and giving up their businesses.

DOES IT HAVE TO BE THIS WAY?

Practices are businesses like any other. The problems you are facing are, at their core, just regular business problems. The medical profession isn't the first to be subjected to major industry shifts.

Across industries, approximately 80 percent of businesses fail within the first five years. Within ten years, 90 percent will close their doors. The odds are against you, but with the right strategy, you can succeed. You just have to know what your business problems are and build a business model and strategy that will help you realize your professional dreams and, by extension, your personal ones.

Physicians running practices face three main problems today:
- Not enough new patients
- Poor reimbursement
- Poor management

At their core, these are age-old problems: not enough new business, tight profit margins, and difficulty retaining and managing staff in a troubled industry. These are real problems, and they should be taken seriously, but once you can name the problems you can start looking for the right solutions.

There is a solution. You just have to relinquish the idea of the traditional practice. This may be hard to stomach, but look at your day-to-day life—you're already nearing a breaking point. You should be looking for proven new business models that can address the problems faced by today's practitioners.

I'm writing this book to inform healthcare providers about just such a model: the wellness center. You have certainly heard about wellness centers. They are fully integrated health centers that combine doctors' offices with other services and amenities, such as a spa, gym, med-spa, physical therapy services, chiropractic services, and much more. They are full-service, one-stop shops where health-minded patients with disposable income can come to deal directly with service providers, sometimes even bypassing the insurance industry entirely.

What's more: a properly built and well-managed wellness center can solve all of your core business problems and restore order, sanity, security, and prosperity to your practice and life. In the next chapter, we'll look at how.

CHAPTER TWO

Owning Your Own Wellness Center—You Can Do It!

If the picture painted in the previous chapter sounds familiar to you, you're not alone. And I know you're not alone, because I have been there. My career as a chiropractic physician has been forged in the same environment, but I managed to overcome the odds and build a successful practice. I want the same thing for you.

My entire career has been based on changing with the ever-evolving healthcare climate and finding a successful model for a medical practice that has the legs to stand the test of time. I took an honest look around and realized that what I was seeing out there wasn't sustainable. It wasn't sustainable because it was a dated business model. The physicians of tomorrow can't have their heads in the sand. They have to understand the lay of the land and build practices that can thrive within it.

21

I have found such a model. The purpose of this book is to share it with other physicians.

After graduating college, I decided I wanted to go to school and become a chiropractor. I worked as an associate for a couple of years and then opened up a private practice in 2003. In 2006, I acquired a small gym. To my surprise, the gym resulted in lots of referrals of new patients to my practice. The gym was actually feeding my practice. I realized then that I could do even better if my practice and the gym were all under the same roof. But why stop there, I thought? What other kinds of businesses might also feed new patients to my practice?

This line of reasoning led me to launch Soul Focus, an integrated wellness center. Located in New Jersey, Soul Focus brings together several specialists under one roof along with a full-service health club and spa. We offer a wide range of amenities and services you can't normally find under one roof.

We offer medical pain management, chiropractic, physical therapy, acupuncture, nutritional counseling, and so much more. We also provide nontraditional services and amenities. You can come for laser hair removal, anti-aging treatments (such as Restyline), Botox, and even laser liposuction. We offer personal massages, facials, kickboxing, yoga classes, and eucalyptus steam rooms. There are tranquility rooms for relaxing, post-treatment foot soaks, and even a couples/party room for enjoying the day together. There's a healthy food bar, juice bar, and more.

The key to Soul Focus's resounding success is that all of these services are offered *together*. Wellness centers are beginning to catch on nationwide, but often people throw the term around like a buzzword. A lot of people call themselves wellness centers, but to be a complete wellness center you need to offer more than just massages within a medical office. You have to create a relaxing, healing environment, the kind of one-stop shop that improves patient health and compliance, client retention, better health outcomes, and, yes, income.

This seamless integration is key to making it work. It creates advantages that answer many of the problems faced by doctors of all disciplines today. In the past, I have worked individually at a posh exercise salon, a med spa, and a medical practice. They had their pros and cons, but none of them came close to a true wellness center. Soul Focus is a symbiotic cross-referral machine, creating a never-ending pool of prospects for every department within the building.

WHY GO AFTER PATIENTS WHEN YOU CAN BRING THE PATIENTS TO YOU?

Doctors today are killing themselves for new patients. As reimbursements go down, taking on more patients is necessary to keep the business profitable. Setting aside that this has you running faster to stay in place, how will you even find these new patients?

Typically, physicians get new patients through referrals from other doctors. Building a solid practice as a specialist takes a lot of referrals. You need multiple physicians working from different offices referring patients to you. This can be a full-time job in itself. These professional relationships take time to cultivate, and you have to continually check in with your referring doctors in order to stay fresh in their mind.

A major drawback to building a business around referrals is that your success will *always* remain in the hands of others. Your practice depends on other doctors continuing to refer to you. If they stop, your practice goes under.

The other way to find patients is to go after them directly in your community. There are many avenues for this. Lunch & learns, health fairs, business expos, chamber of commerce events, PTA school events, and town days are all good venues for getting your name out in the community and building your practice directly. However, most physicians would rather die than have to attend one of these events. It can feel demeaning as a physician to have to do all of your own marketing.

It's also time consuming. These events typically have to be attended on your own personal time because they are usually on the weekends. This can be even more of a grind than keeping up relationships with referring doctors. You may not be relying solely on referring doctors anymore, but you may wish you were.

I built my first practice this way. I went to marketing events. I went to the Chamber of Commerce and networking groups. I marketed myself to other physicians. I did screenings, festivals, and fairs. It was hard work, and I did it on my weekend hours, or early in the morning before work. My practice grew, but it took me away from my family. After a while, it knocked me for a loop. It ran me ragged. It was demeaning and not the life I signed up for when I went to school to be a healthcare provider.

I knew there had to be a better way, and there was. At Soul Focus and wellness centers like it, we don't go hunting for patients *because the patients come to us.* If you build and manage a proper wellness center, they will come to you too.

This may sound too good to be true, but this is one of the prime benefits of opening a wellness center. Patients come to you. The wellness center creates foot traffic right in front of you. No one typically just pops into the doctor's office, but they do when it is in the same building as their local gym or spa.

As a physician, you no longer have to track down patients. All you have to do is build your wellness center and offer the right amenities and services to get prospects in the door. Build it and they will come! They will come for the spa, the steam room, the sauna, the juice bar, the nutrition department, and the tranquility room with a "big screen" aquarium. They'll come for the yoga classes and the health demonstrations. All of these "amenities" are attractive and bring people in the door, and, once in, they come for medically necessary medical services.

This creates a situation in which everyone wins—you, the service providers, and most of all, the patients. The integration is important. Soul Focus is three businesses in one. However, they all function together in a symbiotic and synergistic manner.

This is how Soul Focus operates. There are three primary businesses all operating inside the wellness center: the spa, the gym, and the practice. Each one refers to the others and the businesses all complement each other. Gym members who injure themselves get sent across the hall to the medical office. At my medical practice, patients who finish rehab and physical therapy are sent to the gym to continue their exercise. The spa brings in a lot of foot traffic that benefits the medical practice and the gym.

The best part is that the people who come to wellness centers aren't just prospective patients—they're the *right kind* of prospective patients. They're already interested in healthy living; otherwise they wouldn't be purchasing health services like a gym membership, yoga, wellness/nutrition classes, and the like. They also have disposable income. They do—and they've proven their willingness to spend it on their health.

In today's environment, these are the ideal patients—and you don't even have to go looking for them. They will come to you. Built and managed properly, a wellness center should bring you all the patients you need to keep your practice healthy and growing.

INSURANCE WON'T REIMBURSE? NO WORRIES— WE TAKE CASH!

The number one problem faced by doctors today is declining insurance reimbursement. Doctors have become so dependent on insurance companies that it almost doesn't matter whether or not you join an HMO. Physicians working under the out-of-network model are still at the mercy of the insurance companies, which are instituting larger out-of-network deductibles.

One solution is to start taking cash and other direct payments from patients, bypassing insurance as much as you can. This is a scary proposition for doctors, who generally dislike speaking about money with patients. It's an awkward conversation and can feel at odds with your job to put the patient's health first.

Doctors don't have much experience negotiating with patients either. Historically, insurance companies paid the bills, but this is not the case anymore. Higher deductibles mean that you or your staff will have to talk with patients about the cost of services even when patients do have health coverage.

Thankfully, talking about the price of services is much easier at a wellness center than it is at a traditional practice. For one thing, patients at wellness centers are more likely to feel comfortable paying you directly for services because that's the model of gyms, spas, and many alternative health practices. This makes for an easier transition into a similar relationship with doctors. The patients are in the right setting and frame of mind. It can still be awkward, but less so, and you're more likely to actually make the sale.

Patients who patronize wellness centers are also the right kind of prospects for this. They have the disposable income and the willingness to spend it on health. These are, again, the right kind of patients. Catering to them will allow you to reduce reliance on insurance and into taking more direct payments from patients.

Diversification away from insurance reimbursement isn't a choice you get to make. The health insurance system in this country is unsustainable. It is a bubble that *will* pop and crash. It will look no different than the housing bubble, the dot-com bust, or the 2008 financial crisis. Just as the real estate market and financial industry crashed, so too will the healthcare system. Prices are unsustainably high and still rising, pushing costs through the roof. Patients are starting to wonder what insurance is even for, as they are unable to afford the high premiums and high deductibles.

Eventually the system will break down, and insurance will become unaffordable. The ACA will be unable to pay subsidies for overpriced insurance plans. Medicare will go bankrupt. The writing is on the wall. We don't know exactly what the future holds and can't know exactly how and when this will play out, but we can for sure know that the current system is on the way out. Will the future be a socialized single-payer system as in Canada? I hope not—medical services there are terrible, slow, and inefficient. To top it all off, doctors are paid very poorly. A single payer, or even socialized system like the ACA, will almost invariably result in lower incomes for doctors in traditional practices. It already is.

Act now by moving away from traditional practices.

Wellness centers are the future, and you still have time to get ahead of the curve while also breaking free of your dependence on insurance reimbursement. Forget about insurance. Your new motto: "Cash is king."

Build your business around the add-on services only a wellness center can offer. Your wellness center can become a cash revenue generator that supplements and even eclipses the money you take in from insurance reimbursement. Now you're selling more than your services as a doctor. You're offering gym memberships, personal training, nutritional supplements, spa services, Botox and fillers, laser hair removal, chemical peels, facials, massages, and all kinds of other packages.

Now that's a business model that works—one that isn't dependent on third-party doctors for referrals or insurance companies to make fair reimbursement payments.

A SOUND BUSINESS MODEL

Despite being a more complex business model with many interdependent businesses, a wellness center is actually easier to run than a traditional practice. The business model is custom tailored to today's environment. Soul Focus and wellness centers were designed to operate in the current conditions.

This doesn't mean you can ignore being a better businessperson and managing your staff properly. In fact, it means the opposite—those things become central to your job when you run a wellness center. It means that you can focus on these things without the friction that currently comes with running a traditional medical practice.

Running a medical practice is always hard, but it's harder

when you can't pay your bills because revenue is down and the insurance companies won't pay. Running a practice is harder when you spend all of your time seeing up to five patients an hour, six days a week, fifty weeks a year. Running a practice is harder when your "off" time is spent catching up on administrative work, replacing staff, and trying to find new patients faster than they are slipping away.

On a personal level, it's hard when you spend more time on the phone with referring doctors than you spend with your spouse or kids. It's harder when you can't sleep due to stress.

Make no mistake: running an independent wellness center isn't easy, but it's doable, it's rewarding, and there's a future in it. You put in the work and you see results. You still have to learn to be a sound businessperson. You still have to manage staff and run a business. But you can run it with a *proven* business model.

That model is already available to you. You don't have to reinvent the wheel. Everything you need to do can be found in this book, and we can even help you get started and put you in touch with the right people. This is helpful for most physicians who never learned to run a business the right way because they don't teach that in medical school. They teach you how to take care of patients, not how to run your practice.

You can open a wellness center. You can build a practice that will not have you scrounging for more and more patients who bring in less and less per capita income. You can manage a successful business. You just need to learn how.

The main thing you are going to have to learn is how to better manage and motivate your staff and partners. There will be a lot more staff at a wellness center because you will be offering many more services than before. This can be overwhelming, but subsequent chapters of this book will explain in detail what personnel you need to hire, what they are responsible for, how to manage them, and how to keep them happy so they can keep you happy.

This is what I did with Soul Focus—and you *can* do the same thing. If you're like me, you will refuse the status quo. I wouldn't accept a life in which I had to fight endlessly for referrals and patients. I wouldn't accept that my income would be dictated to me by the insurance companies. And this allowed me to overcome the management difficulties and stresses that come with running a high-volume, low-income practice and, ultimately, build a better one.

THE WAY OF THE FUTURE

The time is right for wellness centers. When I launched Soul Focus, other doctors thought I was crazy, but now these centers are becoming increasingly common and Soul Focus is ahead of the curve, profitable, and now franchising.

We owe some of our success to a public that increasingly recognizes the importance of preventative medicine and general wellness. People today understand that preventing disease means living healthy. This, as much as the changes in the health insurance industry, are making wellness centers a good investment.

The government is helping to pave the way for this transformation. The Affordable Care Act has added provisions that make preventative care attractive to patients by incentivizing them with rewards and have been requiring insurance companies to cover, more preventative healthcare. Insurance companies have begun to pay for services, such as gym memberships. This allows you to reclaim some of your lost insurance reimbursement money and bring in patients from the insurance companies again, all while circumventing the entire HMO referral system! Now insurance companies send their insured to you for prepaid gym memberships. Medicare sponsors a program called Silver Sneakers that will pay for gym memberships. If you become a partnering gym, this can also bring more patients into the office and increase your money from insurance reimbursements ok having to join an HMO for referrals.

Programs like these are just the beginning. In the future, there will be more wellness centers where, instead of paying your monthly premium through an insurance company, you can pay that premium and then buy a membership for your family at a wellness center where all the doctors will be located.

This is already happening today. There are large multimillion-dollar hospital complexes operating under a similar model. Here in New Jersey, there is Virtua Health, in Voorhees, and Centra State Hospital, in Freehold, and more all across the country. Hospitals such as these have built huge fitness centers and spas and started selling memberships. Patients are drawn in by the fact that insurance, now focusing on preventative medicine, encourage and reward for these services.

Hospitals understand that, in the future, they will have to compete harder for patients.

This isn't just for hospitals. You too can make the leap from narrowly focused medical practice to fully integrated wellness center. This may be the *only* way, in the long run, to retain your private practice. The traditional small practice is dying, but small, independent providers can still run their own successful practices—if those practices are wellness centers.

CHAPTER THREE

The Holy Grail: Patients Who Pay, Stay, and Refer

Operating a medical practice today is not like operating a medical practice even a few short years ago. Insurance reimbursements are down. Competition for new patients is greater than ever before. As discussed in previous chapters, practice owners can offset the decline in income by offering cash services. But for these services to be successfully sold, you need to have people to sell them to.

You need to build a loyal and dedicated clientele who will pay, stay, and refer—that's the Holy Grail of the wellness center or any practice. You want patients and guests who keep coming back to your practice for more services, and you want them to tell all of their family and friends about how great you are.

There is no shortcut to building up a happy clientele base that will pay, stay, and refer. There is no trick involved.

But there is a method, and it is simple: **You have to offer real value.**

Patients pay, stay, and refer when they get the best deal at the best price with the best service. It's about quantity, quality, and value. Provide a range of high-quality amenities that people want and they will keep coming through the door. Deliver value and they'll throw dollars at you. Do all of this and they will refer you.

GET THEM IN THE DOOR

The first step to acquiring the right clientele is to get them through the door. We do this by offering not just medical services, but a **whole wellness experience.**

This experience starts the moment they walk through the doors. Upon entering the facility, the soothing sound of running water tickles the ears. Relaxing spa music plays gently in the background. The staff is warm and inviting, but never overbearing. There are massage chairs in the relaxation areas, usually occupied by smiling faces.

We have created an atmosphere that makes people want to stay and keep coming back. It is an oasis of tranquility within the New Jersey suburbs. People come in tired from their busy days. The suburbs here are anything but relaxing. The area is densely populated. There are cars everywhere. Traffic is horrendous. There are lots of good jobs around, but they are mostly high-pressure/high-stress jobs. Many of our guests work in Manhattan and come in agitated from long commutes. They're looking for either a relaxing time in the spa or massage areas, an invigorating workout in the gym, a chiropractic adjustment to get them out of pain, or all of the above.

This is why Soul Focus is so popular. When people walk through our doors, all of their frustrations melt away. They forget about their work problems, irritating commutes, personal problems, and home obligations. We make this our mission.

We pamper our guests while they are with us because we know how hard they work every day. After spending all day focusing on the needs of others, they just need a little time to be the center of attention—to focus on themselves and have others focus on them, too.

The motto at our practice is: "Soul Focus, where the focus is always on you."

This is clear from the moment you enter the office. The space is a retreat, an escape, a getaway. We like to think of Soul Focus as an afternoon vacation—a mini vacation that only lasts an hour or two, but leaves guests feeling rejuvenated and ready to face another day.

This is a big step away from a traditional medical practice. Practice owners have to make a seismic shift away from thinking of their practice as a place to deliver individual services and toward delivering a relaxing, wellness-focused experience to every patient, every time.

THE WELLNESS CENTER ADVANTAGE: UNDERCUT ON PRICE, OUTPERFORM ON AMENITIES

One of today's fastest growing franchises is Massage Envy, a spa club that has eschewed the traditional pay-as-you-go model by offering a membership club with yearly dues. They sell memberships the same way a gym would. Currently, memberships cost around sixty dollars per month. This entitles members to either a massage or a facial each month.

This business model has been fantastically successful. They have experienced phenomenal year-to-year growth. If you live in or near a major American city, chances are you have a Massage Envy near you.

You may think it makes no sense for independent practice owners to offer spa and massage services when popular chains are delivering them at such low prices. You would be wrong. There are limitations to the Massage Envy model that have left a market opening that can only be filled by wellness centers.

One major limitation that establishments like Massage Envy face is location. Most locations are in strip malls. They rent out small storefronts and try to convert them into spas, usually with limited success. Massage Envy succeeds at creating a *spa-like* atmosphere, but they are certainly not real spas. Their practice will never be as relaxing as a real spa due to their location and small size. Their customers must brave traffic to get to congested strip mall locations and then fight for a parking spot in a busy mall parking lot. Then they have to navigate the shopping malls, dodging loud teenagers and hurried shoppers. None of this is particularly relaxing. It is not a true spa experience.

Even more detrimentally, the Massage Envy facilities are less intimate than a traditional spa. They are small storefront venues in a strip mall, and all the décor in the world won't change this. Chimes and scented candles can only do so much. It won't transform a mall storefront into a true spa space. This means that customers will get a massage, but they won't get that extra special spa treatment that drives the industry. People don't go for just a massage—they go to be pampered in a relaxing environment. Massage Envy simply does not live up to expectations.

Yet, they are wildly successful. This is because they don't try to out-compete traditional spas on services or atmosphere. Instead, they compete on price. They undercut the competition by keeping overhead low and passing those savings on to their members. **Their members accept a reduced experience for a lower price.**

This strategy only works if they can keep competing on price. Massage Envy can do this with traditional spas—but they *cannot* compete with a well-run wellness center on price. There are inherent advantages to the integrated wellness center model that make this impossible.

At Soul Focus, we now offer spa memberships at the same price as Massage Envy. We aren't just beating them on price though. We also outperform them with better services and a more relaxing atmosphere. We offer far more amenities than Massage Envy and we do so in a true spa atmosphere. This is possible because we have larger facilities that aren't crammed into a strip mall storefront. The spa at Soul Focus is a true spa, and you get a true spa experience.

We offer locker rooms and showers. (Clients are unable to shower following a massage at Massage Envy!) We have relaxing steam rooms and saunas. We have a tranquility room and a post-treatment room. The final point in our favor is that clients are able to take a class and use our full-service gym on the day of their spa service. This type of space and facility simply isn't in Massage Envy's business model. Even if they wanted to expand, it is likely they could not do so without selling off hundreds of locations and starting over as a business.

Soul Focus can offer all of this for the same price as places like Massage Envy because we don't have to compete on price. The bulk of our revenue comes from the medical practice. The spa and gym are add-on businesses that drive traffic to the medical practice. These add-ons also pay for themselves; making a return from the gym and the spa is just the icing on the cake.

No matter how low Massage Envy slashes their prices, we can always match them. We could literally offer massage services *for free*, operating the spa at a loss, and still use the spa to bolster the Soul Focus bottom line. Every spa member, no matter how little they paid for membership, is a prospect for the lucrative medical practice. There is no way a spa or gym can compete with us on price because we run a more lucrative business. We can afford to operate the spa and gym at a loss if we have to, but a spa or gym not affiliated with a wellness center has to make money solely as a spa or a gym.

Box stores, such as Walmart and Home Depot, have been using a similar business strategy for years. They sell select items at ridiculously cheap prices, often at a loss, simply to get you in the door. They're willing to take a loss on some items in order to increase foot traffic and total revenue. This is what we do at Soul Focus. We are happy to operate side businesses at low margins because that's what they are—side businesses. The medical practice is the cash cow and everything else is in support of it.

This isn't to say the side businesses can't be profitable. They often turn a good cash profit. The gym can at least pay for itself. The spa is likely to turn a profit. Medi-spas are often highly profitable as they sell cosmetic services for thousands of dollars. Customers who care about their looks are very invested in aesthetics. They will often invest thousands of dollars in expensive cosmetic procedures. This can result in substantial revenue—not the kind of revenue a medical practice generates, but a respectable amount that helps offset the decrease in insurance reimbursements.

This is all just bonus revenue. What you really want at the foundation of your customer base are gym and spa members coming through the door and eventually paying for services at the medical practice. This is much easier once you get them through the door. Once they see what a great value you offer, customers are willing to stay, pay, and refer. We make this easy by offering a real value, a sentiment reflected in our marketing campaign tagline for our spa club: **"The easiest decision you'll ever make."**

This is not hyperbole. We offer the best amenities for the best price. Our goal isn't to undercut, but to outperform. For consumers, there's no choice here. Anyone joining Massage Envy would come to us if they were close enough to a Soul Focus and aware of what we offer. The more we get the word out, the more popular we become.

When people hear about our spa and gym membership prices, the first thing they ask is how can we possibly afford to do that. The second is, **"How do I sign up?"**

CREATING VALUE IN THE MINDS OF YOUR GUESTS

The equation for value is quality divided by cost. If you can offer more amenities at the same price, you will have a hit on your hands. At Soul Focus, we are doing this every day. Our integrated practice model allows us to offer more amenities than our competition and bundle them for even greater savings. We offer gym memberships at a third of the price of comparable standalone gyms. It's an unbelievable value. But what really gets them coming back is bundling the gym with everything else.

Bundling services is key to creating greater value. For example, members of the spa club are entitled to use the gym for the day when they come in for their monthly massage or facial. Many of them then convert to being fulltime gym members because we offer a bundled discount for seventy-five dollars a month one gets a massage or facial every month, plus a monthly gym membership. For a small additional fee, only a fraction of what they're already paying for their spa club membership, our spa members can upgrade to a full gym membership. More amenities for the same price, all under one roof—what's not to like?

A well-run wellness center becomes a one-stop healthy living shop. At Soul Focus, we have a juice bar with pressed juice and smoothies. We are expanding it to include warm meals. We offer grab-and-go, gluten-free, organic meals that people can have heated and enjoy at the center, perhaps between their time at the gym and spa, or that they can take home with them so they don't have to cook. The dining area is as relaxing as any other part of the wellness center, with the sound of trickling water and relaxing music.

It's like a home away from home. It is actually nicer than home! Guests are able to leave work and come here for dinner and relaxation. They're able to stop by on a Saturday morning and make a day of it, having a smoothie for breakfast, hit the gym hard, steam, sauna, and finish off nicely in the tiled showers with chromotherapy lights. Grab a quick healthy meal, then spend the afternoon in the spa, capped off by some relaxation time with a book in the tranquility room or the massage chairs. This is not the kind of experience you get anywhere but a top-notch wellness center. **It is an experience only our model can deliver.**

As I wrote at the beginning of the chapter, creating value in the minds of your patients and guests is key to getting them to come, stay, pay, and refer. It's not enough to just offer good services. It's not even enough to offer good services at a good price. You have to also make sure that patients understand that they are getting five-star services at a good price. This means you need to create an atmosphere that matches your product and services.

Consider the case of Planet Fitness, another popular health/wellness franchise, that sells very cheap gym memberships. They are the cheapest standalone gym in the country. They sell monthly memberships for less than most people spend on lunch for the day. They don't have the amenities or services gym-goers expect. They don't have personal trainers on staff. They don't have the state-of-the-art exercise equipment hardcore gym-goers expect. They don't offer showers or classes.

Businesses like Massage Envy and Planet Fitness are successful at what they do, but neither provides a luxury experience. They are going for the bottom of the market, and people expect to pay bottom-of-the-market prices. They deliver amenities and atmosphere commensurate with the prices they are charging. Typically, you get what you pay for, which is what makes Soul Focus such a great value.

At Soul Focus, we don't do bottom-of-the-market. We provide high-end experiences and deliver the right atmosphere and amenities that allow us to charge higher prices. This is crucial to building a luxury brand that costs more. When you go to a fancy restaurant, you know you are going to pay more than at a chain restaurant. Some of this price goes toward better ingredients and some goes toward capturing the right ambiance. You must offer both—you cannot sell high-quality food at a hole-in-the-wall joint or patrons will balk at the prices. You have to provide a nice ambiance if you want to sell high-quality food.

The same is true of a wellness center. If the atmosphere doesn't strike a luxury tone, patients won't care how good your services are. It's not enough to be a good value—you also have to seem like a good value.

In the case of Soul Focus, however, this is all somewhat moot. While *we could* charge higher prices, *we don't*. When it comes to the side businesses, such as the spa and gym, we match our competitors' prices. This allows us to capture maximum market share quickly and generate more traffic to the medical practice.

At the end of the day, Soul Focus is first and foremost a medical practice. It is an integrated medical practice offering lots of amenities and various services, but from a business perspective it operates as a medical practice and that's where we make our money.

STAY ALL DAY—NO REALLY, STAY ALL DAY

You may then wonder—why do we offer all of these high quality amenities and services for such a low price? The answer: because we want patients to come and we want them to stay all day.

Yes, you read that right. We want people to come in and stay for as long as possible. This is the antithesis of how most businesses operate, especially medical practices. Most medical practices maximize revenue by turning over patient treatment rooms much like a restaurant turns its four-tops. They want you to come, drop cash, and get out to make room for the next customer. For all of its talk of creating "a third place" for customers to relax, Starbucks doesn't actually want you to set up shop at their tables all day. That's because you're only going to buy so many scones and pumpkin spice lattes—after that, you're just taking up precious seating that a new customer could use.

Massage Envy certainly doesn't want you staying all day. They want to turn massage tables over as quickly as possible. Or consider your average gym—not only do they not want you staying all day—they would just as soon you not come at all! High-volume/low-cost gyms, such as Planet Fitness, are premised on the belief that 50 percent of their active membership will never show up. Their patrons aren't paying to go to the gym so much as they are for their *desire* to go to the gym. It is better for Planet Fitness if these people pay and never show up at the gym. This means less wear and tear on the equipment and a smaller space that reduces overhead costs. They don't need to invest in trainers and other staff because their members aren't even using them. This works fine for Planet Fitness because they're so cheap—they sell low-quality services, but they do so at a low price that helps them capture a certain demographic of non-gym-goers who wish they were gym-goers.

This is not the Soul Focus model. We are a wellness center, and we care about wellness. If you buy a gym membership and then don't show up for a month, you better believe we are going to have an associate on the phone calling you up to see why.

This isn't merely a business decision—we still get paid whether you use your membership or not. **We care about your wellness.** The gym is just one small part of a larger business interested in total body wellness. We truly want our patients and guests to be well.

We aren't being wholly altruistic here—we also want you coming and supporting the wellness center. We will take the money from the gym memberships, but what we really want is to get you through the door so you can enjoy and purchase our other services and products.

This strategy is at the heart of the integrated medical practice model. Soul Focus offers all kinds of services and products, many of which we've mentioned throughout the chapter. To put it all together, we have a medical office, but we also have the gym, the spa, the medi-spa, the food and juice bars, the multiple relation areas, the massage therapists, the personal trainers, the cosmetics and anti-aging products, the nutritional counselors, the class instructors, and the list goes on!

There is no way a single person could utilize everything Soul Focus has to offer in one day. This means that the longer someone stays at the wellness center, the more they are likely to spend on services and goods. This is why we want our members to show up—it is why we want them to stay all day. **The more they come, the more they stay, the more they will eventually pay.**

The environment is built to encourage people to stay all day. We built Soul Focus like a Las Vegas resort. Resorts and high-end hotels often allow you to use the gym all day when you get a spa service. This encourages you to come and pay for the resort as a whole. They want you to stay because they understand that this is why you're coming in the first place. It is also why you're paying. They want you to use the saunas and sit in the steam rooms all day. They want you to use the tranquility room for hours on end. Their large integrated facilities give them a competitive advantage and they fully leverage it.

We do the same at Soul Focus. Everything is geared toward welcoming guests and enticing them to stay. We want you to come and be yourself and live a small part of your life inside our facilities. We do everything in our power to keep you there all day, including offering free Wi-Fi so you don't have to leave to check email or do business. You can't possibly overstay your welcome with us—unless we are shutting off the lights for the night!

And when a guest does leave, we do everything we can to keep them coming back. We want to operate as a second home. Gyms, massage and spa treatments, healthy food and drinks—these are things that people may want almost every day. Our environment is conducive to encouraging them to come regularly. The more often people come back, the more money Soul Focus brings in. It's a win-win situation when our guests keep coming back and getting healthier and Soul Focus prospers as a wellness center.

IT'S ALL ABOUT THE REFERRAL

The Soul Focus business model relies on word-of-mouth recommendations. Many people don't know about the great value that wellness centers provide. They don't know that they can get a better gym and spa membership for the same price. They don't know the benefits of integrated health systems. We need our members, clients, and patients out spreading the gospel!

Luckily, this isn't hard to do when you're delivering a great service at an unbeatable price. People refer their family and friends to Soul Focus in the same way they recommend their favorite restaurant. When a restaurant delivers great food for less than their competitors, word gets around the dinner table, the neighborhood, and Yelp. The same is true of Soul Focus.

While the medical practice is our bread and butter, we actually get more referrals from the spa and gym. People are amazed that they can get a spa club membership at a real spa for less than they would pay at a strip mall massage joint. Our spa rivals what you might find in Manhattan or Las Vegas—it's a New York experience on a Middle America budget. They're also impressed that our full service gym is so cheap.

These things are probably not as important as good medical care, but they are the kinds of things people are more likely to share over the dinner table and online. People are likely to talk about the cool gym or the relaxing, hip spa they visited. They're less likely to talk about routine physicals, weekly chiropractic visits, or physical therapy sessions.

The quality of experience warrants sharing. No one is going to brag about the cheap massage they got at a chain joint. But they will tell their friends and family about the massage they got at Soul Focus, followed by a complimentary after-treatment service that included a eucalyptus hot-water foot soak while they sat in a massage chair and watched scenery from around the world. They will brag about getting a massage and then retiring to the steam room and sauna. That's the kind of experience that people want to tell their friends about! Other places don't have those amenities, and certainly not at these prices.

There you have it: the secret to finding patients who will not only come though your doors, but also pay, stay, and refer. They come for the amenities. They stay for the wellness center. They refer because you provide real value—which means high quality at a low price. As a practice owner, you can afford to do this because you can provide amenities at a low price while bringing in profits from your now higher-volume medical practice.

The medical practice is where Soul Focus makes its money, but we wouldn't be nearly as profitable without everything else— we wouldn't be nearly as profitable if we weren't operating as a wellness center.

CHAPTER FOUR

The Economics of Running Your Own Wellness Center

The previous chapter explained how a wellness center naturally drives traffic into your medical practice. Not just any traffic, but the *right* kind of traffic that will bring you the kinds of patients who will allow your practice to thrive—those who stay, pay, and refer. They come, they spend, they tell others, and the process repeats.

If you are a practice owner, you have been struggling with declining reimbursement. Your interest is probably now piqued, but you might be thinking of those words made infamous by Tom Cruise in the 1996 film *Jerry Maguire.* "Show me the money."

In other words: What do I really stand to gain financially from opening, or converting an existing practice into, a wellness center? And how do I make it happen for me?

49

SHOW ME THE MONEY

First, let's talk numbers so you understand what is at stake here. The exact level of revenue a practice brings in will vary based on location, specialty, size, facilities, and many other factors. However, we can still look at averages. According to an annual survey put out by UBM Medica, a leading medical publisher, the average income for physicians with an ownership stake in a practice is now under $250,000 and is typically dropping multiple percentage points from one year to the next. This varies by specialty and area of practice. Chiropractors, such as myself, tend to make even less.

By comparison, medical practices operating within wellness centers of the size of Soul Focus can expect to bill anywhere from $2 million to $4 million each year and take home 50 percent of that as profit. This doesn't count any of the amenities. This is simply the boost in income generated from operating an integrated medical practice within a well-run wellness center.

FOCUS ON THE CASH COW

Wellness centers have many ways to boost revenue over a traditional practice. They can offer all kinds of amenities from gym and spa memberships ranging to food and nutrition products. The benefit of the cash money that comes in from these add-ons cannot be overstated. They will supplement your income and help offset the annual declining reimbursements that are now part and parcel with operating a medical practice.

As great as these add-ons are, they are only add-ons. The cash cow of any medical practice is always the practice itself. This is no less true of a wellness center. You will always bring in, on order of magnitude, more revenue practicing medicine than selling smoothies, facials, and gym memberships. Medicine is a high-value, high-margin business.

The practice is worth more because patients are worth more than customers and club members. At Soul Focus, because of the integrated model, the average patient is worth $20,000 per year to the practice. Many patients bring in $50,000 or more. For comparison, the average gym membership brings in $360 to $1,150 annually between membership fees and spending on trainers and other upgrades. The typical spa-goer brings in $1,500 to $3,000 per year from the spa, more if they use medi-spa services.

These numbers are nothing to sneeze at—they add up—but these customers are most valuable as prospective new patients. Patient visits are worth much more than anything else. We bill approximately $750 to $1,000 *per patient* visit and collect about half of that. Why? Because patients see more than one medical provider on their visit. A patient will see physical therapist, chiropractor, and acupuncturist all in one day, or nurse practitioner and nutritionist. These numbers may seem high, but they are reproducible. Soul Focus is good at what we do, but we are not special. We are simply a well-run wellness center designed with patient volume, profitability, and total body wellness in mind.

Our results are reproducible across the country. Any competent practice owner can pull similar figures if they own a wellness center with the right complementary providers, desirable amenities, and facilities well suited to the wellness center model. Follow the principles outlined in this chapter and you too can start building a medical practice that is capable of similar financials.

OPERATE OUT OF NETWORK

Being able to set your own prices is foundational to achieving financial freedom as a practice owner. You have to be able to control prices to control revenue and set your own workflow. HMO networks are killing private practices. Out-of-network physicians routinely bring in more than those that join HMOs. An in-network patient is typically worth *half* that of an out-of-network patient. Providers make only about fifty cents on the dollar for everything you do as an in-network provider.

Worse, this amount keeps going down every year. You will do all of the same work but see your income going down. If you have ever been a practice owner, you already know this—you live it every day.

Many practice owners reading this book, perhaps the majority, are already operating outside of an HMO network. They understand the hardships, but they also understand that working out of network is the only way to make money in medicine today. If you are not already among their ranks, join them now. Free yourself from the tyranny of the high-volume/low-compensation HMO model.

OPERATE WITHIN A WELLNESS CENTER TO FIND THE PATIENTS YOU NEED

Providers only work in-network because they don't know how to find their own patients. HMOs provide a path of least resistance. The HMO provides a steady stream of referrals and advertising. They join the HMO, accept their reimbursement structure, and get listed on the approved in-network provider list. Being on this list means providers benefit from a captive audience.

Of course, the downside is that they give up the right to set their own fees. HMOs are only able to get patients to accept limited options by slashing reimbursement prices. They get patients onto the plan by wringing blood from their network providers.

The beauty of the wellness center is that it frees you from the insurance companies. Wellness centers under the Soul Focus model are a shop-in-a-box model for getting patients in the door, buying services, and referring you to others. This makes advertising a wellness center much easier than advertising a medical practice, but the end result is the same—new prospects walking through your doors every day. You don't have to go after new patients—you can bring prospects to you.

You can't buy this kind of advertising. Television commercials, print ads, billboards—none of these will bring in new patients the way that foot traffic does. None of those traditional methods of advertising work as well for a traditional practice either. Enticing people to come into a gym or spa is much easier than getting them to try a new doctor.

Surround your practice with amenities that get people in the door, get them to stay, and they will buy medical services when necessary. They'll come and stay for the juice bar, the gym, the massage, and the relaxation rooms—they'll return and pay for the medical services.

This is the perfect clientele base because they are health-minded people. Most people go to traditional medical practice because they are sick. People come to wellness centers because they care about health and wellness and they are willing to put their dollars into being healthier. They are healthy, athletic people, but they will actually pay for more medical care than sick people.

They will often need help with pain management, musculoskeletal problems, and sports medicine needs. Be there ready to fulfill those needs onsite by having a practice where they already work out!

OFFER A VARIETY OF SERVICES – INSIDE AND OUTSIDE OF THE PRACTICE

You cannot sell services you don't provide. This is why you should offer as many complementary services as possible. We aren't just talking about the amenities offered by the wellness center and its side businesses. You also want to offer many services *within the medical practice.*

Do this by forming an integrated practice with medical providers of various stripes. An integrated practice at a wellness center may have nurse practitioners, medical doctors of different specialties, chiropractors, physical therapists, acupuncturists, nutritional counselors, and more. These disciplines should complement one another and be aimed at the active, health-minded clientele a wellness center attracts.

This multidisciplinary approach to health care offers advantages to providers, practice owners, and patients—a triple-win! The more medical specialties the practice offers, the more services you can sell and the greater the potential to increase both the average per-visit income and overall revenues.

Delivering more services per visit clearly benefits practice owners, but it benefits the patients as well. These are complementary services that improve wellness. That is the primary reason we all got into medicine—to make people well again.

Everything we do at Soul Focus is designed to deliver on this promise, which is why we operate as an integrated practice offering so many services. Providers operating under one roof can easily function as a team to provide better health care. They are able to consult each other and make in-house referrals rather than referring out. This not only keeps revenue in house, but it also ensures better patient care and compliance. The whole medical team works in concert to deliver quality care.

Patients appreciate how mush easier our model makes their lives. They get better care and they get it all in one place. Rather than having to return for follow-up visits, patients can simply be walked down the hall by staff. They can get multiple referrals and see many providers all on the same day. They can get all of their needs addressed in one visit.

What's good for the patients is ultimately good for the practice. Cross-referrals within the practice boost revenues and allow us to achieve the high per-visit revenue that we enjoy. We bill much more than traditional practices, which simply cannot compete with integrated practices like ours. This is the future of health care.

I saw this firsthand recently when another chiropractor invited me to make an offer on his practice. He was an established physician in his sixties and beyond ready to retire. To many young chiropractors, the offer may have looked like a solid business opportunity. The practice was thriving. He was a good chiropractor with a solid reputation, and he was seeing 150 patients a week. This is a lot of patients and he was turning a good profit.

I did not buy the practice. It was a thriving traditional practice, but paled in comparison to an integrated practice.

Offering only chiropractic services, he was averaging $150 per visit. This is a fair amount, but required him to do all of the work himself to make that income. No wonder he wanted to retire—he was working himself into an early grave trying to keep up with falling insurance reimbursements!

His annual revenue was $230,000 per year. This is nothing to sneeze at, but he could easily have doubled this number by simply bringing in a physical therapist. He was already referring all of his patients out to a physical therapist. If he brought one in-house and started operating as an integrated practice, he could have kept all of those referrals in the practice and doubled his business overnight. He wouldn't have had to do anymore work or expand the facilities.

Had he made space for a nurse practitioner, an acupuncturist, and other providers—effectively converting into an actual integrated practice—the sky would have been the limit!

OPEN A WELLNESS CENTER

Why stop at an integrated practice? Why not offer even more? If he had expanded the facilities and opened up a full-service wellness center, he could have done even better. Rather than doing a half-million per year between him and his physical therapist, he could be bringing in several million per year.

Of course, this is a much bigger upfront investment than bringing in another provider or two. You need bigger facilities capable of housing a gym, spa, and other amenities. He would need to work with a medical doctor or hire a nurse practitioner, and also an acupuncturist, nutritionist, physical therapist, and more—one or two of these wouldn't be enough. I will be the first to admit that opening a well-run wellness center takes time, space, and money—but the long-term payoff is substantial.

An integrated practice operating inside a wellness center allows practice owners the widest variety of services, amenities, and in-house referrals. It offers the greatest foot traffic. It offers a venue where it makes sense to offer the maximum number of complementary services and amenities. You can cross-refer between medical specialties. You can offer massages, acupuncture, gym memberships and access to personal trainers, laser hair removal and anti-aging procedures, and so much more. You can sell products that may not make sense in a traditional practice or even an integrated practice in a typical hospital or office setting.

Wellness centers can sell all kinds of products in every branch of the business. The medical practice can prescribe durable medical equipment, such as braces, orthotics, and take-home therapy equipment, much of which can be reimbursed by the insurance company. The gym can sell smoothies and health food, as well as supplements and vitamins, as can the food bar. The massage center and spa can sell lucrative cosmetics and other luxury products for members to pamper and treat themselves at home, and all of this adds up to boost revenue.

Look to offer high margin items and services where possible: sell high-value medical services in the practice, laser treatments at the spa, micro-abrasion and fillers in the medi-spa, or add high-markup smoothies and protein shakes at the gym. There are many items that can only be offered at a wellness center. For example, personal trainers have a 100 percent profit margin—you let them work independently in the gym and take a cut. Practice owners in traditional practices cannot do this. Think of all the medi-spa services you couldn't offer in a traditional musculoskeletal rehab practice.

There's no end to the possible add-ons and upselling. At Soul Focus, we are always coming up with new services and product lines that allow us to maximize profits by selling more services to the same visitors.

The key here is to keep an open mind and focus on growing your business in any way you can. That's the hallmark of a good practice owner. You're not just a physician. You're a practice owner, which is medical jargon for a *business* owner. The most successful business owners will also be entrepreneurs, always looking for new opportunities, upsells, and ways to improve and expand the services they provide.

CHAPTER FIVE

How to Run an Integrated Medical Practice

I am a true and longtime believer in the integrated medical practice. My first practice, opened in 2003, was an integrated practice. Back then, they were called "multidisciplined offices," but the concept was the same. Integrated practices are built around teams of healthcare providers who, despite specializing in different disciplines, work together under one roof to provide better patient care. Integrated practices are increasingly common today, quickly outpacing traditional sole proprietorships, but the model was taboo at the time.

This was especially true for me as a chiropractor. It was very unusual, and thus difficult, to work in—much less *create*—a medical practice as a chiropractor. The medical establishment frowned on doctors, and even physical therapists, who worked alongside chiropractors. Chiropractic practice was dismissed as a

59

counterculture, to the point that physical therapists were taught that "chiropractors kill people."

Nothing could be further from the truth. The chiropractic profession is an important medical discipline, and its tarnished reputation is the result of slander. The American Medical Association, prior to 1983, regarded chiropractors as "an unscientific cult" and declared it unethical for medical doctors to associate with them. This only changed through the hard work and activism of chiropractors like Chester A. Wilk, who took the AMA to court in a series of trials that stretched from the late 1970s into the early 1990s. A judge eventually ruled against the AMA, which helped to legitimize chiropractic practices. Since then, the profession has come a long way in overcoming the bias against it, but it still lingers today in the minds of some medical doctors and patients.

This bias wasn't, and isn't, limited to chiropractors either. Doctors didn't want acupuncturists or nutritional counselors in their medical offices either. Many doctors took a poor view of any providers who didn't attend medical school. Never mind that chiropractors, physical therapists, and nurse practitioners also go through rigorous medical training—they didn't go to medical school, so they were seen as less serious providers.

For the most part, doctors really only work with other doctors of the same discipline, and preside over nurses and other subordinates. If a patient required care from a different kind of provider, perhaps a specialist in another discipline, the patient was referred out.

These biases stymied the growth of the integrated practice for a long time. Doctors were scared to work with other doctors of different disciplines. They were scared to have mixed-discipline practices. When practices grew, they would hire more doctors of the same discipline and try to see more patients rather than bring in a doctor with a complementary discipline in order to capture their own referrals.

Still, enterprising providers, like me, continued to break ground by opening integrated practices. Today, integrated practices are common and quickly becoming the norm. In the end, we are winning, and we are winning **because the integrated multidisciplinary model of health care just works.**

Integrated practices allow providers from many disciplines to work together as a team. This results in better care, and in return, happier patients. At Soul Focus, our patients repeatedly tell us how nice it is to see their whole medical team collaborating underneath one roof.

What that team looks like will depend on the focus of a specific practice. At Soul Focus, we focus on pain and musculoskeletal medicine. This is often an appropriate focus for a wellness center because the people lead healthy lifestyles centered on diet and exercise. Unfortunately, with exercise and sports comes the occasional injury and pain, and our integrated practice sees many people in chronic or acute pain. At Soul Focus, we cater primarily to these patients.

Given this focus, our integrated practice includes medical doctors, nurse practitioners, chiropractors, physical therapists, acupuncturists, and nutritional counselors. This team works well together in a wellness center. The services these providers offer complement one another and appeal to the kinds of clients who come through our doors and become patients.

In a way, an integrated practice operates under the same strategy as the rest of the wellness center. The practice offers a wide variety of complementary services in the same way that the wellness center as a whole offers complementary amenities.

AN INTEGRATED PRACTICE MUST ACTUALLY BE INTEGRATED

As integrated practices have become more common, the term now gets thrown around liberally. An integrated practice is more than just many providers working side by side. A truly integrated practice has many different kinds of medical providers **working together** under one roof. All too often, purportedly integrated practices place much emphasis on having many different providers under "one roof" while only paying lip service to the part about actually collaborating to with each other.

A truly integrated practice must be just that—*integrated.* Collaboration is the key to success, and bringing different providers into the same room merely facilitates collaboration. Practice owners still need the right processes and protocols in place, as well as proper controls, to ensure that providers actually work together to create synergy. The goal is to create a medical team that is greater than the sum of its parts.

At Soul Focus, we don't just make cross-referrals, though we make plenty of them. Our providers actually work as a team, and we have a process for doing so. We have daily provider/staff meetings. Every morning, the entire medical team meets before we start taking patients. All of the service providers attend—the nurse practitioner, the medical doctor, the physical therapist, the chiropractor, the acupuncturist, literally everyone who is at work that day. Even the front desk staff, the medical assistants, and all others working in the practice attend. In this meeting, we review files on all the patients coming in that day. We discuss their treatment history and current prognosis and come up with a treatment plan before they even show up at the office.

The service providers make decisions in conjunction with each other. This ensures that everyone is fully informed about that day's patients before they arrive for their appointments. The physical therapist knows what the chiropractor is doing. The nurse practitioner knows what they are both doing. This allows us to provide holistic health care that far exceeds what patients expect from a traditional sole proprietor doctor's office. The patients can see and feel this at every step of the process.

DELIVERING TEAM-BASED, MULTIDISCIPLINARY HEALTH CARE

Patients experience our team-based approach from day one. We have a systematic approach to intake that educates the patient and ensures that they receive the benefit of our entire medical team. While every visit will be different depending on how the patient first presents, we have a process in place to ensure patients receive the benefits of integrated care.

New patients typically see several of our providers as they move through the process of initial evaluation, diagnosis, treatment, discharge, and ongoing self-guided care. Each provider has an important role in the process.

The Case Manager

When a patient first walks through the doors of the practice, they are greeted by the case manager who takes the patient's history and symptoms. The case manager is not a receptionist. He or she does more than just intake and process paperwork. (We have a receptionist and front-desk staff for that role.) The case manager is an actual provider, typically either a medical assistant or a chiropractor, able to explain the benefits of an integrated practice.

This job is crucial. Most patients have never heard of an integrated practice and they don't know its benefits. Our case manager explains how the integrated practice works and its benefits, as only a true medical provider can. The patient is given a full tour of the facility, both the practice as well as the entire *wellness* center. We want the patient to know that we believe in preventative medicine and promoting a healthy lifestyle—that, as a wellness center, we focus on wellness, not just treatment. We show them the gym, the massage club, the spa, the medical spa, the health food services—the works. Of course, if the patient is in pain, we may save this tour for later, but most patients enjoy the chance to hear about the wellness center while they wait for their appointment at the practice.

Most patients are beyond impressed by the practice and the center once they understand the reasoning behind this setup. They appreciate our dedication to preventative medicine and holistic health care. They take comfort in our team-based approach to medicine. This is important. The last thing you want is to pass a patient off haphazardly between providers. The patient may mistakenly believe they are getting the runaround and that no one is caring for them, when this couldn't be further from the truth.

The case manager's job is to ensure the patient understands our process and its benefits.

After giving the tour and taking the patient's history, the case manager introduces the patient to the nurse practitioner. This is an in-person handoff. The case manager accompanies the patient to the nurse practitioner and together they review the patient's history and needs with the patient there, also active in discussion.

Nurse Practitioner

Once the case manager leaves the room, the nurse practitioner takes over. The nurse practitioner, not the case manager, is the person who actually directs and oversees the patient's care. He or she administers medical exams based on the patient's history and presenting symptoms and prescribes all medical services. In essence, the nurse practitioner functions as the main general practitioner and diagnostician.

Nurse practitioners can do everything a medical physician can. As a practice owner, it makes more sense to pay the salary of a good nurse practitioner instead of the heftier price of a doctor. This allows you to provide patients with top-notch health care at an affordable price.

Of course, nurse practitioners must operate under a medical doctor's license, meaning that you as the proprietor must either be a medical doctor or hire one who will supervise and direct the nurse practitioner. As a chiropractor, I must work with a medical director at Soul Focus, but franchisees with a medical degree can operate under their own license. This is generally not an issue.

The nurse practitioner starts by performing a full musculoskeletal, orthopedic and neurological exam on the patient, as well as testing for adrenal gland insufficiency (indicator of stress) and a PH toxicity test to see if the patient is too acidic or alkaline, before offering a diagnosis. If x-rays are necessary, we take those as well.

We do all labs, exams, and diagnostics on site when possible rather than referring the patient out for the work. This allows us to control costs as well as keep those dollars in the practice and, most importantly, it is convenient for the patient to have everything done in one office. We don't hesitate to refer out for necessary specialists or things we can't offer—we simply try to offer as much as we can at our own practice. This way, patients don't have to wait on testing or visit other locations, and we don't miss out on revenue we could have captured ourselves.

Patient care and treatment is dependent upon the patient's presentation. Because our focus is pain management and musculoskeletal medicine, most new patients come to us presenting with pain. For these patients, the nurse practitioner orders all the standard first-visit testing, conducts other exams or tests based upon their presentation, and then comes up with a plan to address the patient's pain and other issues.

For severe pain, the nurse practitioner may start by writing a prescription so that the patient can get enough relief in order to start rehabilitation. In general though, we try not to mask pain with medicines, which always come with the risk of side effects. Instead, we first look for underlying musculoskeletal problems and focus on addressing those in order to return the patient to wellness. For this reason, the nurse practitioner generally does not prescribe a treatment plan until after the patient has seen other specialists.

Total Musculoskeletal Health: The Chiropractor and Physical Therapist

After administering exams and reviewing the patient's situation, the nurse practitioner refers patients with pain to the chiropractor if they have skeletal issues, the physical therapist if they have muscle issues, or both if they have musculoskeletal problems. The benefit of having both of these providers under the same roof is that the nurse practitioner can walk the patient down to see the chiropractor or physical therapist immediately. The patient doesn't have to come back for another appointment, which improves patient retention and helps speed up treatment.

Chiropractors and physical therapists are the ultimate pairing for musculoskeletal health care. Physical therapists address problems with the muscles. Chiropractors address skeletal problems. Together, they can help patients address problems with the entire musculoskeletal system that are the underlying cause of much chronic body pain. This pairing lends itself well to an integrated practice model, especially when the medical team also has a doctor specializing in musculoskeletal health that can perform pain management procedures, like epidurals, facet blocks, and other procedures surgeries should conservative therapies fail.

In most cases, conservative therapy is the best first approach and has good success rates. Chiropractors have a great track record of addressing skeletal problems. Physical therapists are used in every hospital in this country to rehabilitate patients. Together, they make a powerful team.

Typically, patients will see the chiropractor first, as skeletal issues tend to be both an underlying cause of nerve pain and often a more direct fix. Most common treatments involve passive care, in which the chiropractor performs treatments on the patient. From there they may be sent to the physical therapist for exercise and rehabilitation.

The physical therapist is likely to offer passive care (e.g., ultrasound, manual therapy, electrical stimulation, etc.) and transition the patient to active care that the patient takes an active role in (e.g., cardio, weight resistance training, etc.). Typically, the physical therapist provides passive care before transitioning the patient into self-managed active care. The physical first reduces muscle spasm, allowing chiropractors to correct underlying spinal misalignments and then helps patients strengthen their muscles, once spinal corrections have been achieved. The final phase of active care involves teaching the patient how to maintain their results in the gym.

Of course, there is no better place to do this than in a wellness center where the gym is just down the hall! Many physical therapists assign at-home exercises to patients upon being discharged from care. Unfortunately, patient compliance with these exercises is low once the patient stops seeing the physical therapist. Having an integrated practice inside of a wellness center improves patient compliance because the patient has immediate access to the gym. The physical therapist can show the patient how to do the exercises in the gym, training the patient on the actual equipment they will use. The physical therapist can then encourage the patient to sign up for a gym membership right there. Once the patient has paid for the membership, they are more likely to keep coming back, especially knowing that their physical therapist is down the hall if they have questions or need a consultation.

Our physical therapists offer a wide range of rehabilitative and strengthening treatments, such as Pilates with a "reformer." Pilates is usually done on a mat, but may also be done on a reformer, an exercise machine with pulleys that adds resistance training to a Pilates routine, which can be used for targeted muscle strengthening to help with rehabilitation. Unlike normal Pilates classes, reformer Pilates can often be covered under insurance as functional medicine since it is prescribed and overseen by a physical therapist.

The Team Meeting

After all the different providers see the patient, they convene to come up with a treatment plan. The physical therapist, the chiropractor, the nurse practitioner, the case manager, and any other provider who worked with the patient will be present to discuss the patient and develop a treatment plan.

This meeting is critical to providing truly integrated care. Providers working in different disciplines often have different diagnoses for the same patient. For example, a patient presenting with back pain may have a spinal alignment issue, muscular weakness, and a sedentary lifestyle due to the pain. The nurse practitioner may only diagnosis the pain. The chiropractor may diagnose the alignment issues. The physical therapist may diagnose the muscle weakness. These diagnoses are all different, but they are all equally valid. They must be addressed in conjunction with one another to come up with the optimal treatment plan.

Our hypothetical patient may be prescribed medication for immediate pain, chiropractic adjustments to rectify the underlying skeletal issues, and then physical therapy to help regain strength. Compare that situation to a sole practitioner who might simply prescribe some prescription-strength NSAIDs before sending the patient on their way with a handful of referrals to see third-party providers for treatment. The patient may feel lost as they navigate multiple providers, none of whom are working together. Compare this situation to an integrated practice where the patient works with one medical team working together. The latter serves the patient better because it provides an efficient, convenient, and superior model of care—all while keeping as much of the revenue as possible in-house.

Providers in an integrated practice come to an agreement about treatment through consensus, but ultimately the nurse practitioner is in charge of approving the final plan. He or she acts as the patient's medical advisor and keeps the process orderly and streamlined.

After signing off on the plan, the nurse practitioner writes scripts for any medicines, physical therapy, acupuncture, nutritional counseling, or other services.

Due to practical considerations, the provider meeting happen, after the patient's first visit. This allows ample time to reach an appropriate treatment plan. The case manager or a receptionist schedules the patient for a second visit after this meeting. The second visit is typically when the providers will, if appropriate, accept the patient for care and present a treatment plan. We don't accept all patients for care—only those we can actually help.

The case manager meets with the patient on the second visit and reviews the providers' findings and decisions. They discuss the treatment plan, and, once the patient approves, we bill insurance or take payment and treatment begins.

The teamwork doesn't stop there though. Our team of providers meets each and every morning to review the patients coming in that day—not just new patients. They discuss each patient's progress and current prognosis and, if necessary, update the treatment plan. Patients who require long-term care are reevaluated in person with all providers periodically, approximately every ten visits, until they reach a state of maximal medical improvement (MMI). At this point, the integrated practice has done all it can for the patient at that time. We use the opportunity to encourage the patient to continue practicing a healthy lifestyle, including proper diet and exercise, by continuing to visit the wellness center for the gym, health food, and relaxation time, while also staying in touch with their medical team.

The Medical Doctor

An integrated practice must have a medical doctor on staff. However, the doctor rarely has to be on-site. The nurse practitioners working under the doctor's license act as the primary care physicians and see most of the patients. The doctor does need to be there regularly if they are also the practice owner.

This does not mean that the doctors won't see patients or add value. At Soul Focus, the medical doctor comes in once or twice a month to see patients for whom the conservative treatment offered by other providers has failed or proven insufficient. The medical doctor performs procedures that the nurse practitioner cannot, such as epidurals, facet block injections, radiofrequency ablations, and other surgical procedures. These are high-value procedures that may be billed to insurance for as much as $20,000, or more. The doctor may only be in the office a couple of times per month, but they bring in substantial revenue and offer services that are crucial to a well-rounded wellness center.

The medical doctor stands to gain much from this arrangement, even if they are not the practice owner. The wellness center and its integrated practice are a source of ongoing referrals. Surgeons and other doctors rely on referrals from other providers. With an ongoing relationship with a wellness center, a doctor can substantially increase their income working just one day a month.

This is why doctors should own their own wellness center. Integrated practice owners not only enjoy considerable referrals from the other providers, freeing them of the tyranny of the HMO system, but they also earn money off the practice itself. They take the lion's share of the practice's revenue, as well as the money generated by the rest of the wellness center. In the case of a wellness center with an integrated practice, this is likely much more than they would make working as sole proprietors in a traditional practice.

Nutritionists

At Soul Focus, we keep nutritional counselors on staff as part of our commitment to preventative care. The kinds of patients we attract through the wellness center are drawn to nutritional counseling. Many of our patients come specifically for nutritional counseling. In a sense, the nutritionist functions as another amenity or attraction for the wellness center, drawing in customers in the same way the gym does.

Nutritional counseling is not usually covered by insurance. However, labs, showing abnormalities in a patients profile, lipids, high blood pressure, or other deficiencies in vitamins or minerals that can be addressed though better nutrition, may qualify for billing insurance as functional medicine.

Patients get coverage for the care they need, and the insurance companies save money. The practice gets to bill the nutritionist's work, (under the direct supervision of our medical department) to the insurance, and more patients are able to afford proper nutritional care.

Acupuncturist

At Soul Focus, we are committed to offering as many complementary services as we can. This is what truly makes an integrated practice. This is why we keep an acupuncturist on staff. Many of the same people who use the spa and medi-spa are interested in acupuncture for relaxation. Like the nutritional counselors, the acupuncturist is a big draw and helps get people through the doors.

Acupuncture is also an important part of our pain management arsenal. Though not fully understood by the Western medical establishment, acupuncture has been around for over three thousand years. In conjunction with Chinese medicine, acupuncture has proven to be effective in relieving stress and pain while improving many markers of medical health. This has been shown in many studies.

THE BENEFITS OF AN INTEGRATED PRACTICE— BETTER CARE AND GREATER REVENUE

The integrated practice is becoming increasingly common in the medical industry because it provides superior outcomes for all parties—patients, providers, and practice owners alike.

Patients benefit from better care and receive multiple opinions as a matter of course. There is no better musculoskeletal care than that provided by a competent chiropractor and physical therapist working together under the supervision of a nurse practitioner and medical doctor, and complemented by acupuncture and nutrition. Integrated, multidisciplinary, team-based care delivers superior and quicker results and better outcomes.

This kind of team also results in fewer repeat incidents of pain. Patients are discharged with a comprehensive plan for self-managed active care focused on achieving a healthy lifestyle based on wellness. When this is delivered within the context of a wellness center, the patient has access to gym facilities in which to continue that care. Once discharged patients tend to be more compliant with ongoing self-care when they have access to a gym right there next to the doctor's office. Greater compliance leads to even better results.

Service providers and practice owners benefit monetarily from integrated practices. In general, an integrated practice will generate more revenue per patient, per patient visit, and overall across the practice, especially when the practice operates within a wellness center. This is because integrated practices can take advantage of in-house cross referrals to boost revenue by keeping billing within the practice.

Integrated practices generate more revenue per patient visit because the patient see, multiple providers on the same visit without leaving the practice. The patient doesn't have to be referred out to see a provider at another location on a different day. We can take care of their needs right then and there. This can boost revenue significantly. On average, chiropractors working alone only bill insurance approximately $150 per visit. At Soul Focus, the integrated practice typically bills insurance anywhere from $750 to $1,000 per patient visit across all providers.

We don't just bill more per visit—we ultimately bill more for each patient in total. This isn't magic. We simply offer more services in our integrated practice. The more services we offer, the more money we make. The patient is also more likely to comply with care when they can see providers all in one day. This convenience improves compliance, which improves both patient outcomes and our bottom line.

The other reason we generate more volume is because we generate more patients. Patients are attracted to multidisciplinary practices. The more services we offer, the more reasons patients have to come through our doors. This is similar to the way Soul Focus generates business in the practice by offering amenities in the wellness center. We follow this same philosophy in the practice itself. The more disciplines we have under one roof, the more services we can offer. Ultimately, more patients come through the door. You will never get a new patient coming in for acupuncture unless you actually offer acupuncture. These are new prospects all providers will have access to, that the practice might have otherwise lost to an acupuncturist down the block.

In combination, these different boosts in revenue can add up to a significant increase in income. This has been true for me as a chiropractor. As a successful sole proprietor working independently, I would be able to collect $150,000, maybe up to $200,000 dollars per year, in income. This is far less profit than the conservative estimate of $2 million net income that Soul Focus generates each year —more than ten times as much as I could have made providing only chiropractic care! This figure only represents the money from the practice itself and doesn't include the cash money generated by the gym, the spa, the juice bar, and the rest of the wellness center.

There is no way I could make this level of income as a sole practitioner, especially as a chiropractor. Chiropractic offices, on average, do far less business than medical practices. This is also true of Soul Focus. The chiropractic department brings in less money than some of the other departments, but as the owner of the practice, I profit from the revenue from the entire practice.

Furthermore, each department—and this includes the doctor's office—brings in more than it would alone because of the internal referrals. Chiropractors may see the most profound bump in income, but many medical doctors can also expand their income several times over by opening a wellness center with an integrated practice. How many M.D. sole proprietors make $2.2 million dollars per year? Some, but certainly not the majority!

Practice owners simply earn more running an integrated practice, especially within the context of a wellness center, than they would as sole proprietors. Medical doctors do well running a practice alone, but they will never make as much working alone as they would if they also offered acupuncture, chiropractic care, and physical therapy. Typically, medical doctors refer these services out, think about how much a doctor refers patients out to others? It can be, and often is, in the millions of dollars. With an integrated practice, they can keep that money in-house. That could be hundreds of thousands of dollars per year for any one of those services.

These results are amazing, but they are not exceptional. We are not special at Soul Focus—**but how we operate is special.** Any healthy, intelligent practitioner with good business sense and the desire to open a wellness center with an integrated practice has the potential to do the same.

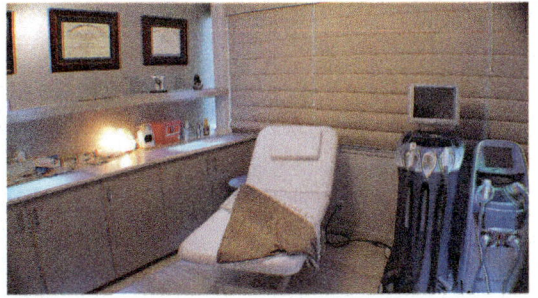

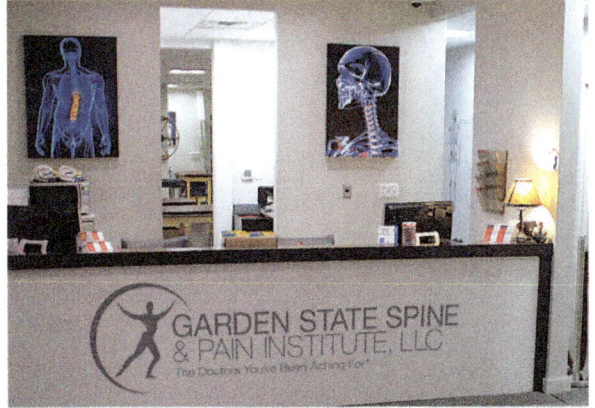

CHAPTER SIX

Creating a Luxury Exercise Salon

The purpose of the gym is to drive people toward the practice. We do this by creating a significant volume of members in the gym and then convincing gym-goers to also become patients. If we run a first-class gym, the expectation is that we also run a first-class medical practice.

This strategy relies on creating a luxury experience for our gym members and prospective members. We have this down to a science at Soul Focus. Creating a luxury exercise salon comes down to just a few things: customer service, atmosphere, amenities, and price.

GREAT CUSTOMER SERVICE—EVERY TIME, ALL THE TIME

You have to create the perfect luxury experience from the moment the customer walks through the doors. This hinges on quality customer service.

Most gyms are impersonal. You swipe your membership card as you enter and no one looks up. No one greets you. No one cares. Not so at Soul Focus! We have staff stationed at an atrium near the entrance to greet people cheerfully. They know our members on a first-name basis. We provide a five-star customer service experience focused on making people feel good. We are constantly praised for our friendliness.

We promote camaraderie between our members. We create an environment where members can help each other in pursuing wellness. Our staff encourages members to engage with each other, as well as the staff. We are trying to build a wellness community. We promote a no-judgment environment where no one feels intimidated as they walk up to the weight machines. People help each other out and our staff leads the way.

Customer service is maintained throughout the entire experience. The gym is well staffed at all times to help members with their needs. When the guest is ready to leave, we collect their towels and ask them to rate their visit. They typically report a top-notch experience, but if there were any problems, we address them on the spot. We make it right—that's the luxury experience.

HOLD YOUR GUESTS' HANDS

Part of good customer service is holding your guests' hands when necessary. Gyms can be intimidating, especially for people just starting a workout routine. You have to be proactive in making members comfortable, as people are often too embarrassed to ask questions about the equipment, exercising, or nutrition.

We make sure guests understand the equipment by taking the time to explain the facilities. Our staff trains them on how to properly use the equipment. We also make sure they are working out correctly. We want them to achieve their wellness goals with getting injured. Upon joining, new members are provided with a TWD consultation. The first is a personal trainer assessment and orientation. Personal training sales generates big bucks with high margins. The second consultation is a nutrition consult which we their eating habits. Our goal is to ensure our members reach their goals in the gym and in life and to provide services to assist them to do so.

CREATING A LUXURY ATMOSPHERE

A luxury ambiance impresses guests and keeps them coming back. Upon entry to Soul Focus, guests are treated to the sound of running water and spa music accompanied by the appropriate lighting to set the mood. The group exercise area has built-in shelves to store the yoga mats and it has beautiful wooden floors. We play relaxing music in the rest areas and workout music in the gym.

We keep the exercise area immaculate. We keep the floors free of dust bunnies. The machines are cleaned after each use to ensure they are clean, look brand new, and are never out of order.

Unlike most gyms that smell like, well, like gyms, our exercise salon smells like a freshly cleaned house. Cleanliness is next to godliness, and our members appreciate being treated as if the facility was prepared just for their arrival—which it was!

CREATING LUXURY

Luxury amenities create a luxury atmosphere. Our luxury gym has a group exercise room, classes, saunas, showers, lockers, relaxation areas, the spa, massage chairs located throughout the greater facility, and a juice and shake bar that also serves healthy meals. These amenities are so popular that some gym-goers visit even on days they don't plan to exercise!

Offer as many amenities as possible and provide excellent service around them. We offer our gym members use of the steam rooms and saunas. We have both a traditional sauna with coals, which is good for a deep, dry heat, and an infrared sauna, which doesn't get as hot but has detoxification properties. People drive for hours to use our infrared saunas. We make sure to have the steam rooms and the saunas already running so they will be hot when guests arrive.

In the gym, we offer a wide range of equipment. We have machines that provide multiple ways of working out the same muscle groups. We have all kinds of cardio equipment, including treadmills, elliptical machines, and bikes.

Broken equipment is fixed or removed immediately. We believe that hanging "out of service" signs on dysfunctional equipment looks unprofessional and ruins the luxury experience. Thus, we work hard to make sure that there is never a machine down, and that if a machine is not working as it is intended, it is removed from the floor. This is maintained through opening and closing inspections, during which any issues are reported and handled immediately. This extra bit of love and care is what differentiates us from other gyms that fail to maintain their equipment.

Hire the right staff to create a truly luxury experience. Your personal trainers are the bread winners. Not only do they get best results for members, they also generate significant revenue with great margins. We also have class instructors who offer classes in everything from spin to yoga, meditation to kickboxing, Zumba to Pilates, and more. These classes run throughout the whole day, every day.

Don't forget that the little touches make a difference. We hand out towels when people arrive so they have them in their locker ready for use. We have plastic bags for people to wrap their sweaty gym clothes in so they don't have to go straight into their bags. In the exercise room, we have a TV on every piece of cardio equipment. We offer cable channels for watching movies, as well as standard stations. We even have our own channel for promoting our services, highlighting staff members, broadcasting wellness-related materials, motivational and inspirational content, and workout tips.

Not all of our amenities are free—we are able to upsell our members every day! We have plenty of grab-and-go health-food purchases. We offer flavored waters, mineral waters, and other drinks at Soulful Café. Guests can grab a juice or shake from the bar. We have organic foods. Some guests order ahead and pick up meals to take home. Some even take home a whole week's worth of meals, each prescribed and handpicked for them by our nutritionist.

We use fine shampoos and conditioners, including exotic ones from the South Pacific, and also offer them for sale. We provide razors, shaving cream, aftershave, mouthwash, Q-tips, colognes and perfumes, hair gel, hairspray, deodorant, and more. We hand select the highest quality products.

ALL OF THIS AT A PRICE NO ONE CAN BEAT

The kicker of course is that we provide this luxury experience and services at unbeatable membership prices. No other gym can afford to provide these services at these prices. The only reason we can afford to do this is because we know that a good portion of the members will also become patients. The gym's margin is not as a profit center—it is an advertising center. We make our money from the medical practice. We have systems in place to encourage members to cross over to the medical practice. Our competitors cannot compete with us because we operate under a different business model.

That business model is based on the cross-referral and the offering of complementary services. Gym members often stay after their workout to get a professional massage, or acupuncture, or even chiropractic services in the practice. They visit our nutritionists. They often become patients—this is the ultimate goal!

Our staff facilitates this process. We have staff members in every business at Soul Focus, including the gym, who inform guests about all the other services our wellness center has to offer. The staff gently encourages them to consider other services. They talk to guests to see what they might want or need. If a gym-goer has back pain, we might suggest chiropractic care, physical therapy, or acupuncture sessions. If they are stressed out, we suggest use of the massage chairs or perhaps even a professional massage or facial in the spa.

We make sure to recommend complementary services that are right for the guest. We don't want them to feel like they are being pressured. We want them to feel spoiled while taking advantage of the luxury experiences Soul Focus offers.

CHAPTER SEVEN

Designing the Perfect Spa

A luxury spa is just as important to a full-service wellness center as a luxury exercise salon. Both are key to the Soul Focus business model. Many of the principles that apply to creating a luxury gym also apply to the spa.

DELIVERING A LUXURY ATMOSPHERE

At a spa, the luxury experience is your product. This is what you are selling. Guests are there to be pampered and made to feel like royalty in the lap of luxury. If you are not delivering this experience, you are failing as a spa. Give them luxury service because nothing less will do.

This focus on creating a luxurious therapeutic environment can be observed throughout the spa at Soul Focus. It can be seen from the moment guests walk through the doors. We provide state-of-the-art amenities. The spa facilities, including the locker rooms and saunas are outfitted with chromotherapy lights. These are special therapeutic lights that slowly shift from red to blue to green and have been shown to provide a physiologic relaxing effect on the body.

Customer service cannot only be good—it must be lavish. When guests arrive at the spa, they are greeted and provided with a nice, clean, fluffy robe, comfortable slippers, and a warm towel. They are then escorted to the locker rooms where they are provided a short tour of the amenities. They then get undressed, put on their comfy robes, and store their things in the combination lockers.

We encourage spa guests to arrive at least a half hour early. This gives them time to make use of the saunas, steam room, and showers prior to their service. This allows them to relax and unwind before their treatments. The massage is relaxing in its own right, but relaxing beforehand allows guests to better enjoy the experience. If they come in stressed out, as most people do, their massage will be almost over before they relax enough to actually enjoy themselves.

This is so important that, while we encourage them to come early enough to use the saunas and steam room, we require them to spend fifteen minutes in the tranquility room. This is essentially the waiting room. This is no typical waiting room like at the doctor's office. It is part of the whole luxury package—part of the experience itself, just as much as the massage. No one minds spending time in this room. In fact, they are nearly guaranteed to enjoy themselves. The tranquility room is so relaxing that spa-goers often return after their service to spend more time relaxing here.

The atmosphere of the tranquility room lives up to its name. Everything is tranquil and serene. The contemporary and sophisticated décor creates the tranquil and serene appearance. We have an elephant, a symbol of good fortune, in almost every room. A wall hanging display small circular mirrors stretch nearly floor to ceiling. Guests can recline on plush chaise lounges or take a seat on the wing chair and prop their feet up on the ottoman. There is a fireplace, a nice touch during an East Coast winter. There are afghans for guests to wrap around them if they get cold. The coffee tables are beautiful and made of small circular mirrors, which create a sense of aesthetic cohesion with the wall hangings. It is a soothing environment and everything is just perfect.

There is no chromotherapy in this room. We have other things for guests to focus on, such as magazines, various bottled waters, teas, and healthy snacks, or a big-screen television that plays relaxing aquatic scenes. Guests are escorted in and allowed to get comfortable, enjoy a cup of tea or snack, and relax while soaking in the atmosphere.

We all but require them to spend the full fifteen minutes here before their treatments. The goal is to get them to lower their defenses so that they can relax before their massage or facial. They may have just left their busy, high-stress workday, or perhaps they are taking an hour or two away from the kids. Whatever the case, they need help unwinding *before* their spa service.

After their time in the tranquility room, the spa esthetician or therapist escorts the guest into a Zen-like treatment room for their service.

The treatment rooms are just as serene as the relaxation room. They have beautiful silver-mesh flooring and backdrops behind the counters. They have their own vanity and sink and built-in touches. They are also equipped with chromotherapy lights. The rooms give the sense that everything has been put here by design for the guest—which is exactly the case. Everything about the experience and interaction is meticulously thought out and managed.

GOOD PROVIDERS RESULT IN GOOD TREATMENTS

Of course, the real draw is the massage. There is little to say about this, from a business owner's perspective, except this: hire only the best massage therapists, because second best is not good enough.

At Soul Focus, we only hire world-class massage therapists. They must have previous experience working in a spa environment, and we do check references. We expect them to have a client base already built up, as this is a sign of a talented massage therapist. We also expect them to have the same friendly and inviting personality we expect of all of our staff providers.

The same holds true with the estheticians who provide facials and other cosmetic services at Soul Focus. These too are provided by only the best-trained, most-experienced providers.

In short: when it comes to delivering the best treatments, you need the best providers.

THE POST-TREATMENT ROOM

An hour-long professional massage is very relaxing—so relaxing that it can leave guests feeling loopy afterwards. They are left in a blissful daze, which, while pleasant, can be very intense. They may feel woozy, as if they have spent a pleasant day at the beach drinking margaritas in the sun.

After such an experience, guests need quiet time to come back to reality. Unfortunately, most spas simply take you straight from treatment to the showers, before nudging you out the door. The staff may start chattering and asking you questions before you are even ready and capable of speaking. This can be a real mood killer when you just need a moment to collect yourself.

At Soul Focus, we don't want our guests feeling woozy. We certainly don't want them feeling stressed out after their massage. We want them to bask in the afterglow of their massage or facial.

We have created a space for just that. After the guests receive their treatments, they are escorted to a post-treatment room. Here they are given a space to come back to Earth, metaphorically speaking, before quite literally returning to their daily lives. This is a relaxing space where guests enjoy large comfortable leather chairs with a basin filled with warm water for a foot soak. We scent the water with various oils, such as lavender, eucalyptus, and peach, whatever the guest prefers. Another large-screen television is playing nature and landscape scenes from around the world.

Guests are allowed to stay in the post-treatment room as long as they like, but most people only take ten to fifteen minutes, about the time it takes for the basin of water to cool down. This is usually enough time to come back to reality, allowing them to reenter the real world—albeit far more relaxed and serene!

After leaving the post-treatment room, guests are free to spend more time in the tranquility room if they want. They are free to use the gym, showers, steam room, and sauna. Remember, the

Soul Focus business model relies on keeping people in the wellness center as long as possible. We welcome guests to stay as long as they may like and try to create an atmosphere that actually encourages them to do so.

The post-treatment room allows guests to leave the spa in a more collected state of mind. This has the added benefit of returning them to a personal place where they might want the other services the wellness center has to offer. They may now be ready to do some yoga or go for a quick run on one of the treadmills.

OFFER WHAT OTHERS CANNOT

The main draw may be the massage or facial, but it is the built-in extras that really set our spa ahead of the pack. Every spa worth its salt will provide excellent massages and facials in a beautiful and relaxing environment, but few, perhaps none, offer the full experience that Soul Focus does.

I have traveled far and wide visiting spas, and none of them (unless they are associated with a large, expensive resort) provide spa-goers with the opportunity to use a gym for the entire day of their spa service.

The tranquility room and the post-treatment room also set Soul Focus apart. They are not add-ons, but part of the actual experience. They don't cost extra, and guests really appreciate the extra touches. This goes a long way in creating a luxury experience. A good massage is a good massage—but a Soul Focus massage is so much more. We pamper you before your massage and help you come down afterwards.

Very few spas and salons offer such a well-rounded experience that both readies the guest for their spa service and then brings them back down to Earth. Most have waiting rooms, but not a tranquility room. I have only ever seen one other spa with a post-treatment room.

Most spas do not have large enough facilities to recreate our experience and, even if they did, they could not operate it profitably. Spas operate with very low margins. Standalone spas must make their money on massage and facials. Offering the services and amenities we offer would put them out of business. We are only able to do this by running the spa as part of larger wellness center in which we make our money off the medical practice.

THE MEDICAL SPA—WHERE THE REAL MONEY IS MADE

Delivering luxury massages is gratifying. Unfortunately, it is not very profitable. Traditional spas are low-margin businesses. The services do not generate much revenue, the labor costs are relatively high, and the cost of constructing so many extra rooms can eat into the meager profits of a spa. It can take years for a newly constructed spa just to break even.

However, these are nonissues for a wellness center. The spa's main goal is to drive traffic into the practice. It does not have to be profitable on its own. Breaking even is good enough, especially if it is drawing a large number of patients into the medical practice.

That said, the spa can generate considerable income. The way to do this is by including a medical spa inside the spa. The spa can send guests over to the practice for medical care, but it can also provide medical procedures of its own right inside the spa facilities.

These services do require a cosmetic medical provider or trained nurse practitioner on staff. At Soul Focus, the medical spa has a medical provider on staff who offers Botox, fillers (e.g., Juvéderm, Restylane, etc.), and other cosmetic procedures. We also do laser refraction of skin, laser hair removal, laser lip, and other cosmetic services.

None of these services are reimbursable through insurance. This is not necessarily a bad thing. Insurance reimbursements are going down and medical practices need to start generating more cash income to offset the losses.

A medical spa is a wonderful tool for doing just that. The services provided at a medical spa are not cheap. We offer Botox at $500 to $750 per session. Laser hair removal can bring in thousands of dollars per patient for large areas like the back or legs. Fillers are also profitable and require ongoing maintenance.

These services can really add up if your staff is good at upselling. There are a variety of services that can be provided. None of them are necessary, but people pay big money for vanity services. On average, the medical spa brings in $500 to $1,000 in revenue per visit. The cosmetic doctor can see four patients in an hour, potentially bringing in $4,000. Compare that to the $100 to $150 in revenue from a facial and massage that lasts an hour, and it is easy to see how adding a medical spa can make any spa much more profitable.

Finding a cosmetic doctor to work with is not difficult. We have a renowned cosmetic surgeon, well known in his field, delivering services at our medical spa. He has his own practice, but benefits from working with the wellness center by picking up patient referrals for elective surgical procedures. Your cosmetic doctor may bring in a few thousand dollars performing fillers and Botox at the wellness center, but these patients are worth far more to him as referrals. Your cosmetic doctor or surgeon will likely have their own practice where they perform much more expensive procedures, such as liposuction and plastic surgery. This makes it well worth their time to spend a few hours or days a week picking up new patients at your medical spa. It is a win-win situation that will make their practice better as well as your own.

CHAPTER EIGHT

The Synergistic Cross-Referral; The Gym Fills the Practice; The Practice Fills the Gym

The secret sauce of the wellness center lies in getting all of the many businesses to work together synergistically. Simply running several businesses under the same roof will not substantially increase the bottom line of the medical practice. Running a gym and a spa, as standalone businesses are not worthy of this type of investment. However, getting the gym and the spa to function symbiotically with the medical practice can result in a substantial boost to revenue to a medical practice operating on its own.

You want all of the businesses to work together as a single machine. The practice is the engine, but the other businesses are integral to the wellness center model. You cannot drive across town with only an engine. You need the brakes, the steering column, the carriage, and all the other parts that make up a car. It is only when they are assembled together that the engine will carry you across town. This is how we think of Soul Focus.

99

The gym, the spa, the medical practice, the juice bar, the food bar, and all the relaxation stations and amenities around Soul Focus are part of the same machine. They do not simply operate under the Soul Focus badge, but they function as a unit. The people staffing each business collaborate to meet our guests' needs and the needs of the wellness center as a whole. Soul Focus is not several businesses under one roof. We are many businesses operating together as one, providing wellness.

Achieving this level of integration and synergy across the entire wellness center is neither easy nor automatic. The natural inclination of most, new wellness center proprietors is to focus solely on the practice. This seems logical and practical because the practice is the cash cow. The practice shoulders the financial responsibility of the entire wellness center and without the practice, there is no wellness center. There is no reason for the other businesses to even exist without the economic engine.

It is only once the practice is up and running that new wellness center proprietors start paying attention to the gym, spa, and other businesses. Again, this makes logical sense because the purpose of the other businesses is to drive traffic to the practice. While the hope is that they will become self-sustaining and even turn a profit, this is not their primary purpose. It is entirely possible to operate the side businesses at a loss as long as the practice does well. For this reason, new proprietors may be tempted to ignore them while they get the practice up and running.

The problem with this approach is that it results in the proprietor running the wellness center as several different businesses. The business processes are not integrated and the businesses do not function symbiotically. They operate under the same roof, but they do not operate together. Each may each benefit from the foot traffic that the other businesses generate, but there are no systems and procedures in place to seamlessly cross-pollinate in an intentional and optimized manner.

Developing and implementing protocols and processes that drive cross-referrals between the businesses is the secret to creating a symbiotic environment. The wellness center is not made up of separate businesses operating under one badge because the whole point is for them to work synergistically. They must be set up and managed in a way that makes this not only possible, but standard operating procedure. Collaboration must happen from the top and all the way down. The businesses should "talk" to one another, preferably from the day they open.

Most owners are so focused on getting the different businesses to function that they fail to focus on the main goal: generating cross-referrals. The cross-referral is the key to the wellness center model. It is the secret sauce. It is the whole reason for opening a wellness center in the first place. As the owner of a wellness center, the cross-referral is your greatest tool for driving cash sales from outside the insurance reimbursement model, enjoying higher patient loads, achieving greater patient retention, generating more revenue, and netting greater profits. Cross-referrals are the goal of and sole purpose of Soul Focus wellness center.

HOW THE GYM FILLS THE PRACTICE

Though gyms can be highly profitable businesses, their success brings in significantly less revenue than a successful medical practice. Gyms make money in two ways: gym memberships and personal training. Selling gym memberships typically provides only enough revenue to keep the lights on, the machines in working order, and other operation costs covered. Personal training is where most traditional gyms make their money. Personal trainers are paid a cut of their services from the gym owner and personal training has high revenue margins. This is profitable, but pales in comparison to the kind of money that can be made in a medical practice.

Nonetheless, gyms are staples of the wellness center model because they attract affluent individuals who are interested in healthy lifestyles. This is your target demographic as a practice owner, particularly at a practice that focuses on musculoskeletal care, pain management, and sports medicine. Gym-goers are most valuable to a wellness center as prospective patients.

The true value of the gym is in generating referrals to the practice. Set up and manage the gym in a way that reflects this fact. While foot traffic to the gym will naturally migrate over toward the practice, the most efficient way to move gym-goers toward the practice is through referral. The prospective patient should be made aware of and guided toward medical services that would benefit them. This is best done by developing business processes that will automatically screen gym-goers for medical needs that can be met at the practice.

The gym staff should make gym-goers aware of everything the wellness center has to offer. When people come to the gym at Soul Focus for the first time, they are given a tour not only of the gym, but of the entire wellness center. Our staff explains the wellness center model, how the gym fits into a broader healthy lifestyle, and the benefits and conveniences a wellness center offers. Gym-goers typically make for a captive audience precisely because they are health-minded.

This initial tour is the first sales pitch that new gym members receive, but it is not the last. New gym members are given two appointment dates. The first is for a free health assessment with a personal trainer. The personal trainer measures the new member's percentage of body fat and collects other health markers. The new member is then given a free consultation with the personal trainer. The trainer works with the gym member to develop a custom-tailored exercise plan.

The goal here is twofold: We are trying to sell personal training packages, but we are also screening for medical needs. If any abnormalities show up on their assessment, the personal trainer can refer the member to the practice for further screening and medical services.

The second appointment is a free consultation with our nutritional counselor. The nutritionist helps the new gym member develop a meal and supplement plan that focuses on total wellness. The nutritionist analyzes their body fat results, adjusting for skeletal muscle mass and water weight, and determines how much weight the person needs to lose or gain.

The nutritionist also recommends tests to measure blood pressure, lipids, and other health measures. The nutritionist explains that, while nutritional counseling is not covered by insurance, functional medicine often is. Abnormalities in the member's blood work might allow them to get their nutritional counseling reimbursed by insurance as part of an overall functional medicine provider. This is generally enough incentive for the prospect to want to undergo testing.

This is a great way to immediately convert gym members into patients at the practice. The nutritionist or personal trainer refers the patient to the nurse practitioner for lab work. The nurse practitioner then orders any necessary labs and sets up an appointment to review the lab results. At this point, the gym member is now already in the practice!

Members are fully screened for any health concerns and receive a customized diet and exercise plan that considers their personal needs as measured by our medical team. If their lab results show any problems that can be addressed by diet and exercise, such as abnormal lipid profiles, they may be able to get all of this covered by insurance as part as functional medicine program. If not members pay for services in cash. This is a great service and shows the convenience and benefits of a wellness center! This alone is enough to make a gym member a patient for life and our physicians become doctors again, often getting patients off of their blood pressure medication, diabetic insulin, or cholesterol meds. Everyone wins!

This gym-to-practice pipeline functions remarkably well when it is built into the business model. Our system gives us at least three early opportunities to convert a new gym member. Between the initial tour and the two free consultations, gym-goers, have three chances to see the medical practice, as well as the spa, medical spa, juice bar and meal station, and other amenities.

These tours are really sales pitches with a personal touch, and this means that our staff has to be trained as salespeople. Our personal trainers and nutritionists understand the services offered at the other businesses so that they cannot only upsell within their division, but also make referrals to the other businesses. They are adept at identifying potential patients who would benefit not only from more exercise and better nutrition, but also from acupuncture, chiropractic care, physical therapy, and other more expensive medical pain management procedures offered at the wellness center.

At the end of the day, the goal isn't just to sell gym memberships—the goal is to upsell services to better serve the members' needs. We want to drive the members toward the practice and also keep them coming back to the wellness center to enjoy the many amenities offered. The value of the gym is not the money made from gym memberships, or even from personal training. The real value of the gym is that it gets people in the door and keeps them coming back to use the exercise equipment, receive personal training, undergo nutritional counseling, and enjoy in the myriad of benefits of a wellness center. Many of those benefits are found at the medical practice. Our staff seizes every opportunity to remind gym-goers of this fact. The gym is set up to feed the practice.

HOW THE SPA FILLS THE PRACTICE

The spa drives new prospective patients toward the practice in much the same way as the gym. Selling spa memberships is not very profitable, but it does cover operating costs. Much likes the gym, the spa is not the cash cow, but unlike the gym, the spa is profitable and generates significant income from the medical spa and cosmetic services. The spa's job is to attract people to the wellness center and to offer amenities that keep them coming back. Our affordable spa club program entitles members to a monthly massage or facial, which keeps them coming back to the wellness center on a regular basis.

The ultimate goal is to upsell medical cosmetic services to

spa-goers and convert them into patients at the medical practice. Our staff is trained to evaluate the spa-goer for potential medical issues. For example, people often come in for a massage precisely because they already have back pain. We train spa workers to identify any musculoskeletal issues and recommend the spa-goer to the practice for a free consultation. This gets them into the practice, where they can become patients and be evaluated for any underlying spinal or muscle problems that are precipitating their back pain. The massage is important palliative care, but they ultimately need to address the underlying medical problems.

While the spa does provide a respectable overall profit for Soul Focus, we are happy to take losses on individual services if they keep people coming through our doors. Our number one loss leader at the spa is laser lipo. This is an amazing weight-loss procedure that uses lasers to heat up and liquefy fat deposits in the body. The procedure can shed inches off the thighs, waist, and other areas quickly. Keeping the weight off requires a proper diet and exercise, but the weight loss jumpstart is often what people need to get excited about a healthy lifestyle. This can be the incentive they need to keep the weight off, and we facilitate this by referring them to the gym for a membership.

We offer low-priced laser lipo sessions in order to generate strong foot traffic. These people are prospects who get the same tour we give gym-goers. We walk them through the entire wellness center facility, explain the benefits of the wellness center model, and give them the same sales pitch we give gym-goers. This is often enough to get them to sign up for our spa club or a gym membership.

Laser lipo nicely complements our business model. It

is performed over several sessions over the course of many days, which means that clients have to keep returning to the wellness center. They also have a strong incentive to join the gym. In fact, they will have the opportunity to exercise in the gym after each of their laser lipo sessions. This is because of how the procedure works. The technician uses lasers to heat up the fat until it liquefies. There is only a small window of time before the fat will solidify. Patients need to use this time to drive the fat toward the lymphatic system for excretion. The best and only way to do this is through exercise.

This makes having a gym down the hall extremely convenient. The technician performs the procedure and then takes the patient to the gym to spend twenty minutes on an elliptical or treadmill. This is a prime opportunity to let the patient try out the gym. This also gives us twenty minutes to upsell them other complementary services, such as a weight-loss program with our nutritionists or sessions with a personal trainer.

Our staff is trained to upsell. They explain that laser lipo can help shed fat, but keeping it off requires diet and lifestyle changes. We explain the merits of nutritional counseling and encourage them to sign up for a gym membership and personal training package. Many spa-goers love the gym and our trainers. They often become members, stick around, and eventually seek out services at the medical practice on an as-needed basis.

They are also very interested and easily upsold to the many cosmetic medical services we offer in the medical spa. They may want more laser lipo. They may sign up for regular acupuncture sessions, one of our more popular spa services or, they may be interested in the services performed by our cosmetic surgeon. We offer Botox, facial fillers, acu-facials, laser hair removal, and laser skin refractioning. These are all high-value, profitable services that allow us to recoup the losses on the laser lipo and then some.

Just as with the gym, the primary goal of the spa is to get people in the door, keep them coming back, upsell them other services, and funnel prospective patients toward the medical practice. Spa club memberships and affordable laser lipo are just two ways of accomplishing this task. We are always devising new ways of attracting prospective patients through the spa and gym and upselling them more services and generating new patients for the practice.

AMENITIES, AMENITIES, AND MORE AMENITIES

As Soul Focus has grown, we have offered more and more services and amenities. We have expanded beyond the three core businesses of the practice, spa, and gym into a full medical spa with acupuncturists, physical therapy, and cosmetic surgery. The more services we offer, the more people we bring in, and the more cross-referrals we can generate. The more services and products you can offer at the same place, the more the average patient is worth and the more you attract the masses.

We have added more actual side businesses, such as a juice bar and a food bar, that also drive foot traffic. People pop into the bar to grab a healthy lunch or dinner. They may want a healthy shake or cleansing juice. Much of this food is grab and go. Customers can preorder prepared meals and pick them up for the week. They can be stored for a few days, so regulars may pick up as many as five meals at a time. This keeps our busy customers stocked in healthy food they don't have to cook. Rather than going home to cook, they can hit the gym for an hour after work and go home with balsamic glazed chicken, quinoa pilaf, and a kale salad. This is not cafeteria food, but healthy meals laboriously prepared by our third-party vendors. It's fast, it's delicious, it's healthy.

The food and juice bars work synergistically with the rest of the wellness center. Healthy food is part of a healthy lifestyle, and at Soul Focus, everything is fresh and most of the meals offered are organic and gluten free. Our nutritionists are able to recommend meal plans that we can actually prepare and deliver at Soul Focus. The food and juice bars can actually refer people to the nutritionists and vice versa.

The people who stop at the food bar are no different from any other prospect. We have staff on hand to give them the same tour of the facilities as anyone else. If they aren't spa club or gym members, we try to sign them up. We are happy to show them the medical practice. Of course, we respect people who are busy and on the go, but they often want to tour the facilities and see what we have to offer.

There is a natural cross-pollination that takes place here. Just as a nutritionist can refer patients to the nurse practitioner, the front desk help can refer customers to the nutritionist. We focus on healthy food, making this handoff natural. Our staff is trained to talk not only about the juices and meals for sale, but also our exercise programs, personal training, spa services, and everything the wellness center has to offer.

We are always looking to expand Soul Focus in new ways and develop new programs to attract and further engage people. We do events and special programs. We offer loyalty programs, such as punch cards that entitle guests to a free service after a certain number of paid services. We throw parties and community gatherings. We sometimes offer complementary massages, free gym days, and other giveaways.

All of these events are opportunities to make cross-referrals. We often hold events simultaneously in order to cross-pollinate between different sides of the business. We want spa-goers to try the gym, gym members to try the spa, and everyone to learn about the medical practice. We always have staff on hand to give tours and explain what we do. They are able to sell or upsell services on site. This stimulates cross-referrals and emphasizes how all the businesses at Soul Focus don't just operate under the same badge, but actually complement one another. People see this and begin to fully appreciate all of what the wellness center offers.

IT'S ALL ABOUT THE MEDICAL PRACTICE

As important as synergistic cross-referrals are, referrals from the practice to the other businesses are less crucial than referrals that move people toward the practice. This is because the whole goal of the wellness center is to generate foot traffic and memberships that will bring people into the medical practice. Once someone has become a patient, the goal has been reached. You don't open a wellness center to get rich off the side businesses. You open a wellness center to enrich and grow the medical practice.

However, we do regularly make referrals from the practice to the other businesses as a matter of course. Those services truly improve our patients' lives. We work with people suffering from muscle and spinal pain. These people benefit from the pain and stress release that results from a massage or facial. They benefit from strengthening core muscles in the gym. Everyone interested in wellness benefits from a proper diet and healthy meals. The synergy between the services we provide across Soul Focus is not manufactured—it is real and the benefits are genuine.

Making referrals to the gym and spa also benefits the practice. Patients who sign up for the spa club come back at least once a month to receive their spa and facial. When patients sign up for the gym, they may use the facilities several times a week, if not every day. This keeps them coming back to the wellness center on a regular basis. Keeping them in the system ensures that they will think of us first when they need the medical services we provide. We want our patients to keep coming back. We want them to be patients for life.

At Soul Focus, we have a system in place for handling patients that delivers quality care and complies with insurance company preferences. We automate cross-referrals by building them into the business model. We want patients to use everything the wellness center has to offer. In order to get the service they do at Soul Focus, patients would have to travel around town between four or five different locations. We capture revenue that would be referred out by solo practices. Patients would much rather be referred down the hall for a same-day appointment than across town or to a specialist who might not have an opening for weeks or months.

Our system for handling patients and referring them to different services at Soul Focus is designed around the kinds of patients we most typically see. Most of our patients suffer from musculoskeletal ailments and pain. They are typically in too much pain to exercise or even perform normal daily activities. We usually start them in passive care that is mostly palliative. The goal here is to reduce their pain so that they can start active care.

The wellness center gives us many in-house options for palliative passive care treatments. We can refer patients to the spa for deep tissue massage. We can schedule them appointments with our acupuncturists. We can send them to the gym or a personal trainer for light stretching exercises. We have numerous treatments in the practice, including ultrasound, electro-stimulation, heat, ice, medications, and other treatments.

Once the pain and inflammation subside, we move patients into active care. This includes exercise under the direct supervision of the physical therapist and eventually a personal trainer. These active treatments are meant to rehabilitate and strengthen the muscles that are causing the injury and pain. Because we operate in a wellness center, we can send the patient to the gym to work with personal trainers and physical therapists to come up with a treatment plan. The patient never has to leave the facility, and we are able to monitor their progress and adjust the plan as we go. Our practitioners, physical therapists, and trainers can work together to develop and execute a custom-tailored exercise plan for each patient.

The size of our facility allows for many options. We have free weights, weight resistance training and cardio. We can set the patient up on bands for isometric exercises, or sign them up for a gym membership so that they can continue their rehabilitation and maintenance exercise program on their own at Soul Focus. All the while, they have immediate access to our entire medical staff and our personal trainers to help prevent further or additional injuries during rehabilitation. This requires shuffling patients between providers. Done carelessly, this can confuse or upset patients. We are careful to always hold the patient's hand during the entire process. Our nurse practitioners work closely with the physical therapists and personal trainers. The nurse practitioner will review the patient's test results with the physical therapist in front of the patient. The same thing is done when the physical therapist hands the patient off to a personal trainer. Whenever a patient is moved from one provider to the next, their history and needs are reviewed in front of the patient. In the medical practice, we also meet every morning to review that day's patients together. Collaboration and full integration are key, especially when the medical practice is working with the providers in the gym and spa.

Managing patient handoffs is crucial to the wellness center model. When the physical therapist hands the patient off to the personal trainer, the patient is given a full tour of the wellness center. They may have been offered a tour previously, but may have been in too much pain to take it all in. By this point, the patient has undergone passive care and is in less pain. They are ready for active care and are now able to appreciate and use all that the wellness center offers. The personal trainer gives them a tour of the whole facility, including the gym where they will exercise.

We hold their hands through the whole process, guiding them through passive care and pain management, interventional care, and then active/physical therapy rehab. We then ease them into a new, healthy lifestyle that includes a proper diet and exercise. Nearly everything the patient needs can be provided at the wellness center, making us a one-stop wellness shop. Anything we cannot provide in-house, we refer out and check in periodically so that we can be the ones managing the patient's health plan.

Once the patient has been referred to the gym by the medical practice, the personal trainers and gym representatives take over. At this point, the patient's care is usually no longer covered by their health insurance. They will often need to continue doing exercises to strengthen muscles, but insurance companies do not usually reimburse the patient for these costs. It is up to the gym representatives to convince the patient to buy a membership and/ or personal training package. This is often an easy sell. The patient now trusts us and understands that their healthcare providers are just down the hall. They know they need to do the prescribed exercises and that there is no better place to do them than in the same facility as their medical team.

As the proprietor of a wellness center, cross-referrals are your lifeblood. You generate them by getting all the businesses to function as a unit. You want the businesses and the people staffing them talking and collaborating. You need to set up processes that ensure that upselling and referrals are baked into the business model. The gym and spa aren't there just to run as businesses — they are conduits for moving people toward the medical practice. The businesses should synergize and actually function as one business model.

This strategy is part of the wellness center ethos. Everything we do at Soul Focus is aimed at creating a cohesive experience for all of our guests and patients. The atmosphere should be relaxing across the entire facility. The businesses should be set up in a way that breeds collaboration. You want guests to see the different businesses. We have Soul Focus set up around an atrium that opens up onto all of the businesses. They can see the gym and the spa. They can see the medical practice and the food and juice bar.

Guests are referred from one business to another. They see the personal trainer from the gym working with the physical therapist from the practice. They understand why the nurse practitioner is recommending them to the acupuncturist. They are working together with the nutritionist, their doctor, and their trainer to come up with a diet and exercise plan that meets their medical needs.

This cohesion creates both a strong business model and a cohesive experience for guests. When people see the different businesses working together to improve their lives, they will keep coming back and tell all of their family and friends. The wellness center will grow, referrals will come in, and the practice will do better.

This is the secret to making a wellness center function properly. A wellness center is not an assortment of businesses under one roof and ownership, but a single organism with many parts. The number one misstep new proprietors make is running the businesses independently. The whole purpose of opening a wellness center is to drive cross-referrals and drum up business for the medical practice. Do this, and your wellness center will by wildly successful and well worth the effort. Soul Focus is verifiable proof.

Raj Gupta

CHAPTER NINE

Can I Really Afford This?

This book is not a sales pitch. The wellness center sells itself. My goal is to provide information about what has worked for me as a practice owner. The benefits of a wellness center are obvious for anyone to see. Wellness centers operating with an integrated medical practice are the future of private-practice health care in the United States.

The old system no longer works—not for patients and certainly not for practice owners. Across the country, doctors, chiropractors, and physical therapists in private practice are working more hours but making less money. They are seeing insurance reimbursements go down. They are getting fewer referrals and worry they will have to give up their autonomy, join an HMO, or sell their practice to a large hospital group. Their private practices are stalling, shrinking, and sometimes even failing. They don't know what to do.

The wellness center solves all of these problems for practice owners. Wellness centers generate extra cash income that can offset falling reimbursements. Wellness centers generate more revenue by bringing in foot traffic and generating cross-referrals within the business, thus alleviating the need to join an HMO network or sell their practice. Wellness centers also generate more money per patient and per patient visit, which allows practice owners to get off the hamster wheel. They don't have to keep working harder and longer hours for less money.

Upon recognizing the benefits of running a wellness center, many practice owners have only one reservation. They don't know how they could afford to open a large wellness center with a full-service gym and spa facilities. This is an understandable concern because wellness centers seem very big in comparison to traditional practices.

It is true that opening a small practice requires far less overhead, and all you need is office space with a reception area and an area to see patients. Depending upon the type of practice you are running, the investment in equipment is small compared to setting up a wellness center that includes a full gym with all the exercise equipment. However, the greater payoff of the wellness center is undeniable. The investment is large, but it is also financially sound.

In the end, this is not really a choice you get to make. Over the long term, traditional practices will suffer more and more. There will come a time when they can no longer survive, and it will be necessary to cut overhead and eliminate staff. Nor will they be able to compete with the new wellness centers popping up in every city. Traditional practices are drying up and disappearing. Those that get in ahead of the curve will be able to establish themselves as the next wave of practice owners.

The question, then, is not whether you can afford to open a wellness center. The real question is—how can you afford not to run an integrated practice as part of a wellness center? The economic landscape has changed drastically for doctors and other healthcare providers in this country—and it has changed for the worse. Practice owners far and wide face the same situation. They can choose to react passively or proactively.

The majority of practice owners will remain passive and accept the lower reimbursements and falling income. There is nothing wrong with this choice, but recognize it for what it is. This is a choice to accept that your business will continue to operate under an outdated business model and will bring in less money every year. Eventually, you may no longer be competitive at all and may have to retire your career as a practice owner and either work for someone else or hang up the stethoscope.

If you have factored a lower income into your future and can accept these terms, then there is no reason to read this book. If you can accept that your practice may one day become obsolete and even unprofitable, feel free to put this book down right now. You have accepted your situation honestly and managed to make peace with it.

If you're like me, you find this situation unacceptable. You didn't go for years of schooling to make less money every year. You want to provide good care while earning a better living. You see the changes in the healthcare industry and are ready to adapt to the new lay of the land. You are open to new ideas and business models that may look radically different from how you are accustomed to operating—so long as they help you keep your private practice and remain profitable.

Many practice owners feel this way. They are not okay with their income going down. They do not want to remain at the mercy of the insurance companies as they slash reimbursements. They refuse to join an HMO. They want to retain their autonomy, regain control of their future, and get back in the driver's seat. These people are the target audience of this book. I want these people to reach out to me and help create the medical practices of tomorrow.

We now know what these practices will look like. They will be integrated practice models based around offering more services. They will operate within larger facilities that offer multiple complementary services. More and more hospitals are already operating this way. They are bringing in more types of providers and offering more services and amenities. Small practices need to do the same. They need to partner with other providers who provide complementary services. Additionally, they need to offer more amenities by opening complementary businesses within their practices. This is the practice of the future.

The future will look different for different practices. For those working in sports pain, physical therapy, musculoskeletal medicine, and similar fields, the answer is to open a wellness center. Gyms, spas, and health food stores will complement your practice and help it grow in these challenging times.

FINANCING OPTIONS

Opening a wellness center is not cheap and the cost can vary wildly based on location, the ability (or inability) to expand your current facilities, and your particular needs. There is no set cost because there is no single wellness center. The model is flexible.

You may not need, or even want, to build a gym as large as the one at Soul Focus to still reap benefits from the model. There are many other adjustments that can be made.

Nonetheless, opening a full-service wellness center requires a substantial upfront investment to build the necessary facilities. The facilities need to be nice and in a good location. Ideally, you will have enough space to spread out and open many new side businesses, which can quickly get expensive. The return is well worth the investment, but the initial outlay can be substantial.

There are ways to raise the necessary capital even if you don't have the cash on hand. Banks are always looking for good small business investments, and this is definitely just such an opportunity. Soul Focus is a registered franchisor and a proven brand, and the wellness center is a proven model. We have a working relationship with several banks that know our model and how we work. They recognize our proven methods and know we are a profitable franchise.

This can make getting a loan to open a Soul Focus franchise faster and easier than trying to open your own independent wellness center. Lenders are often more careful about lending capital to new businesses and they want to work with people they know. Competent business owners can still get loans to start a business under their own branding, but the process is more difficult. Not only do you have to prove that you are a competent businessperson, you also have to prove that your business model works.

This isn't the case with a Soul Focus franchise. The franchise and franchisor are already vetted. The bank is now simply evaluating the franchisee and the new location. This makes the financing process much easier than trying to open your own new business. All you have to do is prove that you can run a franchise at the chosen location. The bank knows that you will be working with people who developed the business model and know how to implement it successfully. Of course, you don't have to go through our banks. You can apply for a loan at a bank or other lender that is already familiar with you. We can work with you to bring the lender up to speed on what we do, how we do it, and the success we have realized at Soul Focus.

You may also want to consider a loan from the Small Business Association (SBA). The SBA provides advantageous loan programs and terms to new businesses and small entrepreneurs. Soul Focus is also a registered franchise listed with the SBA. They know what we do and work with us and our franchisees to open new locations. They offer great programs and terms to businesses like ours.

We are currently investigating an SBA product catering to business owners who will occupy the entirety of their building. Under this program, they offer better loan terms. These loans are well suited to the wellness center model and can help you acquire standalone facilities large enough to house an entire wellness center.

Partnering with other providers is another option for raising the capital and easing your own financial burden. Partners can pool funds, lowering the upfront investment for each partner. Having more partners and collateral often means better financing terms from the bank, which can lower your overall costs.

Partners also provide other benefits. The right partner is a business asset. Partners who are providers operating in a complementary field are particularly valuable because you get the expertise of the partner without having to hire more staff. Medical physicians can partner with chiropractors or physical therapists and operate practices under the same roof. This is great for generating the necessary cross-referrals that make a wellness center profitable.

Your partner doesn't have to be a provider. You could partner with a gym owner or spa owner or other businesspeople interested in the wellness center model. You don't have to be a healthcare provider to run a wellness center. Many entrepreneurs and businesspeople bring a lot to the table without having to actually deliver services at the practice.

Whatever your situation, there are financial options available to you. A wellness center is a good investment and you will be able to find partners, lenders, and funders if you look in the right places. We can easily put you in contact with banks that are already familiar with Soul Focus, our brand, our business model, and our outstanding financial success. If you would prefer to go through your own bank, or seek out an SBA loan, we will work with you to facilitate the financing process in any way we can.

The costs of opening a new wellness center are considerable. But the cost of not opening one is greater. If you are reading this book because your practice is making less and less money each year, then you already know the price of *not* doing something now.

GETTING STARTED *TODAY*

You do not have to open up a full wellness center to start implementing some of the principles and methods outlined in this book. We encourage practice owners to test out some of the ideas starting today.

The wellness center model is rooted in the premise that offering complementary services and amenities will attract prospective patients to the practice. These places are the perfect side businesses for drawing in health-conscious people with disposable income. Ideally, you would set up a full gym and spa on-site at your practice, but this requires having enough space to do so.

However, you don't *need* a full gym or spa to start offering services commonly found at gyms and spas. Many of these services are complementary to a medical, chiropractic, or physical therapy practice. You can offer some of them at your offices to start bringing in new foot traffic now.

Use the space and resources already available to you. Many spaces can be transformed into spaces for new purposes. Designate a room as the exercise room and start offering yoga and Pilates classes. This doesn't take much space. You can offer evening classes after the practice closes or on the weekends if you have to. The waiting room could be transformed into an exercise room at the end of the day. If you have an area dedicated to physical therapy, this space could be used to have classes or even a small gym with a few pieces of workout equipment for patients to train on. You could partner with a personal trainer and allow them to operate at your practice in exchange for cross-referrals.

There are also ways to expand the practice itself. If you don't have room for a spa, consider a medical spa. This can be set up inside the practice simply by offering new services. You don't even need a cosmetic surgeon to offer basic procedures. You can hire technicians to perform laser hair removal, anti-aging procedures, birthmark and spider vein removal, and other simple procedures. Many of these services are offered in medical facilities already, so patients are not surprised or uncomfortable to receive them in your office. I did this early in my career by buying a few lasers for my office. This was a simple investment that brought in new clientele who paid in cash and often wanted for my chiropractic services, also.

Once you build up a clientele base for the medical spa, you can perhaps start offering therapeutic massages on certain days. Step by step, you can expand the services you offer and the amenities you provide.

This is the trick: Start small taking your first step. Then take the next, then the next, and so on. There is no limit to the number of ways that you can start bringing in prospects at the practice by offering services not typically found at a medical practice. If these services are highly targeted at the right demographic, you will be able to convert some of these people into new patients.

This will extend the reach of your practice while also bringing in side cash money, which are the main goals of a wellness center. They are best and most easily realized within the context of a wellness center, but you can get a taste of what owning a wellness center has to offer by implementing a similar strategy on a smaller scale in facilities you already own.

Ideally, of course, you really want the space to separate side businesses from the medical practice. You want space for a gym and spa. A full gym will attract more people than an exercise room. It is always more relaxing to get a massage at a spa than at your doctor's office. The more space you have, the richer the experience you can provide.

For these reasons, all practice owners should make operating a wellness center a long-term goal. This is the future of health care in America and across the globe. You cannot afford to cling to the past. Your practice, your livelihood, and your future as a practice owner ride on your ability to be proactive and forward thinking.

Raj Gupta

CHAPTER TEN

What Are the Next Steps?

The world has changed for practice owners. The old rules don't apply and yesterday's models no longer work. The practices of tomorrow won't look like the practices of today. Practice owners must adapt to changes in the insurance industry and the larger healthcare system.

In the future, virtually all practices will be integrated practices. Many will integrate the practice into a larger business model, which is why wellness centers are the future of private practice. For the innovative and entrepreneurial early adopters, they are the private practice of *today.*

I have made it my mission to not only open wellness centers, but to help them proliferate across the country and the globe. After seeing the economic success and positive patient outcomes at Soul Focus, I would be remiss not to share the model with others. It would be borderline unethical—a violation of the Hippocratic oath! I want to help preserve private practices by helping them evolve so that, ten or twenty years from now, we are not in a situation where all healthcare providers have joined large HMOs or worse, sold their practices, and patients are forced to receive impersonal health care from large, faceless medical centers staffed by overworked and underpaid medical staff.

This is why I wrote this book, but it only scratches the surface of how to design, open, and operate a wellness center. Wellness centers are complex businesses that can take on many forms. A wellness center is made up of many other businesses that must both function on their own and synergistically as a whole. There is no way a single book could contain a full blueprint or all the practical knowledge necessary to run a wellness center. There is no way I could impart all of what I have learned, mostly by trial and error, in these few pages. This book is only the tip of the iceberg.

Consider this book as an introduction to the concept. For those who want to learn more, you can reach out to us at Soul Focus. We give free lectures, seminars, and tele-seminars for those medical physicians, chiropractors and their entrepreneurs interested in learning more about wellness centers. We cover an array of topics, including business location, employee agreements, hiring and firing, training, department and system setup, and more.

We even do private consulting for those interested in opening their own wellness centers. We work with medical doctors, chiropractors, and physical therapists who want to open their own practices, or those who are already in private practice but want to increase their earnings. On occasion, we even work with entrepreneurs who are not healthcare providers but who believe in the wellness center model.

In order to help people get started, we encourage them to download a free report called "Secrets to Opening Your Own Wellness Center." Inside this free report, you will find a step-by-step guide to opening your own wellness center. We detail real strategies currently being used at Soul Focus and by other leading practitioners who are "rocking it" every day—ethically, effectively, and, frankly, while having a great deal of fun.

Inside this free report you will find information on these topics:

- How to find a location
- How to find financing
- How to negotiate a lease
- How to set up your legal structure
- How to design and equip your wellness center
- How to find, train, and retain providers
- How to implement services and profit centers
- How to provide excellent service that turns your clients into raving fans
- Our secret cross-referral system that turns your clients from each business into lifetime customers who partake in all services, including high-value patient services
- And much more!

The "Secrets to Opening Your Own Wellness Center" free report will literally equip you with the best path to success for yourself, your practice, your family, and your clients. It is the perfect companion to this book and the next step in moving forward with opening a wellness center and reclaiming your practice, your career, and your life.

Download your free step-by-step outline and battle plan for opening up a wellness center at www.SoulFocus.com/franchising.

Don't put your future on hold. The future of health care is here today.

Sincerely yours,
Dr. Raj Gupta
drraj@soulfocus.com

CPSIA information can be obtained
at www.ICGtesting.com
Printed in the USA
BVOW07*1255310517

484902BV00001B/1/P